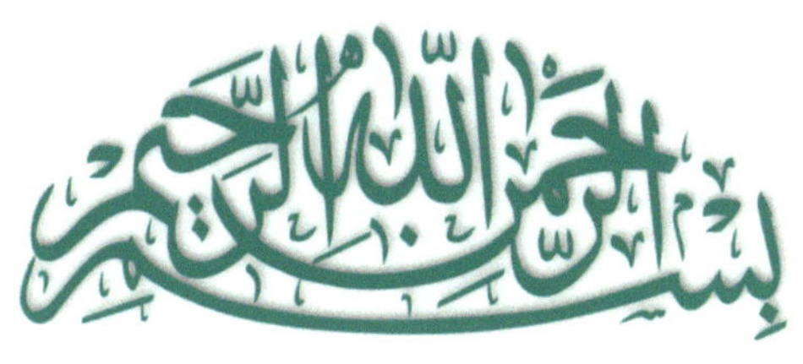

Guided by Authentic Sources and Scholarly Insights

Special Edition

NUR OF TRUTH

MD SAIFUDDIN

Copyright

image credit: ia5e

About Author

Md Saifuddin is a passionate knowledge seeker of Islamic teachings, with a deep interest in exploring and compiling knowledge. While research is his primary focus, he enjoys writing as a hobby, using it as a means to present Islamic principles in a clear and thoughtful manner.

In Nur of Truth, he brings together foundational Islamic knowledge, moral insights from the Qur'an, and discussions on common misconceptions to provide a well-rounded perspective for readers. His work aims to inspire understanding, reflection, and a deeper connection to Islamic teachings.

Through his research and writing, Md Saifuddin hopes to bridge knowledge gaps, encourage meaningful discussions, and contribute to the spread of authentic Islamic wisdom.

image source: pexels

Acknowledgement

With utmost gratitude, I begin by thanking Allah, the Most Merciful and
Compassionate, whose guidance and blessings have illuminated my
path.
I am deeply indebted to the profound teachings of Prophet Muhammad
(Peace be upon him), whose wisdom and exemplary life continue to
inspire and guide countless souls, including my own.

I would like to express my heartfelt appreciation to my beloved parents,
family, and all others who have shared their knowledge with me. Their
unwavering support, love, and encouragement have been the
cornerstone of my strength and determination.

I extend special thanks to Imam Md Shahzad, whose invaluable
guidance and insights have enriched my understanding and
significantly contributed to the completion of this work. His wisdom
has been a beacon of light throughout this journey.

image source: pexels

Table of Contents

Introduction

"Nur of Truth" provides guidance based on authentic Islamic sources and scholarly interpretations. It presents Islam as a way of life centered on submission to Allah and the pursuit of peace. The core beliefs include the Oneness of Allah, the finality of Prophet Muhammad (PBUH) as His messenger, and the guidance derived from the Qur'an and Sunnah.

The book explains the Six Articles of Faith, which form the foundation of a Muslim's belief system: belief in Allah, His Angels, His Holy Books, His Messengers, the Day of Judgment, and Divine Decree. While it briefly touches upon the Five Pillars of Islam, the book emphasizes adherence to divine principles.

"Nur of Truth" introduces important figures in Islamic history, including the Prophets who conveyed Allah's message and the Companions (Sahaba) of Prophet Muhammad (PBUH), whose lives of faith and sacrifice offer invaluable lessons.

Additionally, it covers the ethical and social dimensions of Islam, highlighting the rights and duties that Muslims hold towards their parents, relatives, and neighbors. The book draws attention to the timeless morals derived from the Qur'an, providing guidance for navigating life with justice, kindness, and compassion.

Ultimately, "Nur of Truth" underscores the comprehensive nature of Islam, guiding individuals towards a just and moral existence grounded in divine principles and the teachings of Prophet Muhammad (PBUH) and his companions. By exploring these essential elements, this book aims to provide readers with a clearer understanding of Islam's core tenets and its enduring relevance in the modern world.

Foundations of Islam

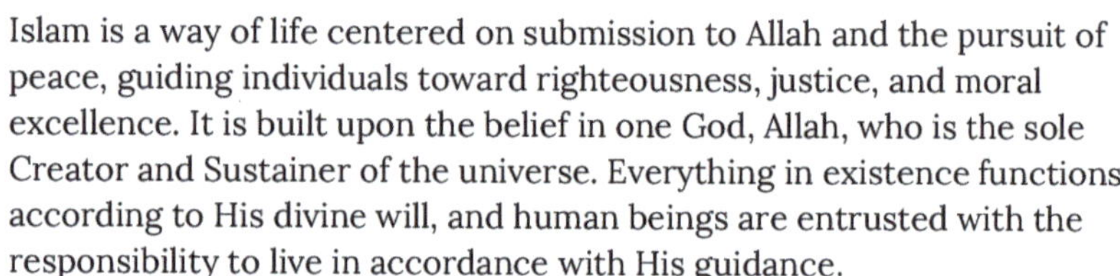

Definition of Islam

Islam is a way of life centered on submission to Allah and the pursuit of peace, guiding individuals toward righteousness, justice, and moral excellence. It is built upon the belief in one God, Allah, who is the sole Creator and Sustainer of the universe. Everything in existence functions according to His divine will, and human beings are entrusted with the responsibility to live in accordance with His guidance.

Muslims believe that Prophet Muhammad (peace be upon him) is the final messenger of Allah, sent as a guide to lead humanity out of ignorance and toward divine enlightenment. His teachings and practices (Hadith) serve as a practical model for living a righteous life. The Holy Quran, considered the literal word of Allah, provides the ultimate source of wisdom, instructing believers in faith, morality, and the principles of justice.

Islam emphasizes the importance of maintaining balance in all aspects of life, advocating for social harmony, kindness, and the well-being of individuals and communities. It teaches that righteousness is not confined to rituals alone but is reflected in character, honesty, and compassion. Fairness, charity, and the protection of human dignity are central values, encouraging believers to support the needy, uphold justice, and treat others with respect and humility.

The faith encompasses six fundamental beliefs: faith in Allah, His angels, His revealed books, His messengers, the Day of Judgment, and divine decree. These beliefs shape a Muslim's perspective on life and responsibility. Islam also prescribes five essential acts of worship, which include the declaration of faith, prayer, charity, fasting, and pilgrimage. These practices are not just obligations but serve as a means to purify the soul, develop self-discipline, and strengthen the connection with Allah.

In essence, Islam is about complete submission to Allah's will, seeking knowledge, living with integrity, and striving for a just and moral existence. It provides a framework for inner peace and societal harmony, guiding humanity toward a life of purpose and fulfillment.

Who is Allah?

Allah is the Supreme Creator and Sustainer of everything. In Islam, He is the one true God, without equals or partners, and the only one worthy of worship. His attributes are perfect, as described through His 99 names, including the Most Gracious and the Most Merciful.

The Qur'an describes Him clearly: "He is Allah—there is no deity except Him, the Knower of the unseen and the seen. He is the Most Compassionate, Most Merciful. He is Allah—there is no deity except Him, the Sovereign, the Pure, the Perfection, the Bestower of Faith, the Overseer, the Almighty, the Compeller, the Supreme. Exalted is Allah above whatever they associate with Him." (Surah Al-Hashr 59:22-23)

To understand why there must be a Creator, imagine a hanging chain where each link is held up by the one above it. If this continued infinitely with no anchor point, the entire chain would never be suspended—it would simply fall. For the chain to hang, there must be a final, unshaken anchor holding it up.

Similarly, if everything in existence depended on something else before it, with no ultimate independent source, nothing would exist. But since we do exist, there must be a self-sustaining, uncaused being holding everything together—Allah, the Absolute.

As Surah Al-Ikhlas states: "Say, He is Allah, the One. Allah, the Absolute. He begets not, nor was He begotten. And there is none equal to Him." (112:1-4)

Allah alone is eternal, self-sufficient, and the source of all existence.

Who is Prophet Muhammad (PBUH)?

Prophet Muhammad (peace be upon him) is the final Prophet that Allah Almighty sent for the guidance of humankind. He was born in Makkah and received the first revelation from Allah when he was forty years old. Following this event, he devoted the remaining twenty-three years of his life to preaching Islam.

Even before receiving the message of Islam, Prophet Muhammad (peace be upon him) was known among his people for his honesty and truthfulness. He was well-behaved and loved and respected by those who knew him, earning the title Al-Ameen (the trustworthy) due to his sincerity and integrity.

At the age of forty, Allah blessed him with Prophethood, and he began to preach Islam, starting with his close relatives as commanded by Allah. He called people to worship Allah alone and to abandon the worship of idols. His mission faced significant opposition and cruel persecution, particularly from his own tribesmen. Nevertheless, he persevered in spreading the message of Islam and eventually migrated to Al-Madinah, where the Muslim community flourished.

Muslims believe that Prophet Muhammad (peace be upon him) is the last of the Prophets sent by Allah. His traditions and sayings (Hadith) are recorded and are considered vital sources for understanding and implementing the teachings of Islam in daily life. He is seen as possessing the highest character and serves as the best example for all people to follow. Deeply loved and respected by his Companions, he treated others with mercy and patience. His life and teachings provide the ultimate guide for Muslims in all aspects of life, leading them from darkness to the light of guidance.

What is Qur'an?

The Qur'an is considered the literal word of Allah and serves as the divine book followed by Muslims worldwide. It is a revelation from Allah, often referred to as the Noblest Qur'an and the Noble Qur'an. The Qur'an was revealed to Prophet Muhammad (peace be upon him) over a period of 23 years, beginning when he was forty years old.

Muslims believe that Allah Himself has guaranteed the protection of the Qur'an from corruption. Additionally, the Qur'an has been preserved through the memorization of countless individuals.

The Qur'an stands as the clearest sign of Prophet Muhammad's (peace be upon him) prophethood, with Allah challenging both humans and jinn to produce a single verse like it, a challenge they have been unable to meet. It is regarded as a great and everlasting miracle.

The Qur'an includes narratives of past prophets and their communities, such as Nuh (AS), Hud (AS), Salih (AS), Abraham (AS), Yusuf (AS), Musa (AS), Sulaiman (AS), Zakariya (AS), and Isa (AS).

It offers guidance on various aspects of life and calls people to worship Allah alone, warning against turning away from its teachings. Verses from the Qur'an were recited to kings, such as Najashi, and have inspired individuals like Umar bin Al-Khattab (RA) to embrace Islam.

The importance of the Qur'an was underscored after the deaths of many who had memorized it; Abu Bakr ordered its collection to ensure its preservation. During the rule of 'Uthman bin 'Affan (RA), efforts were made to standardize the recitation of the Qur'an in the dialect of the Quraish, and he was reciting the Qur'an when he was killed.

The Qur'an is described as a book in which the verses are explained in detail, written in Arabic for those who understand, providing glad tidings and warnings. It serves as a reminder for those who fear Allah.

What is Sunnah?

The Sunnah in Islam refers to the practices, actions, and sayings of the Prophet Muhammad (peace be upon him). It serves as a practical interpretation and application of the Quran, guiding Muslims on how to live a virtuous and righteous life according to Islamic principles.

Understanding the Sunnah is essential for Muslims, as it complements the Quran by providing real-life examples of how to apply its teachings. It helps clarify Quranic verses that may be broad or ambiguous, offering context and making it easier for believers to implement these teachings in their daily lives.

By following the Sunnah, Muslims also uphold the traditions and preserve the legacy of Prophet Muhammad (peace be upon him). It serves as a moral compass, offering guidance on various aspects of life, from personal conduct to interpersonal relationships.

The primary source of the Sunnah is the Hadith, which consists of narrations that meticulously document the sayings, actions, and approvals of the Prophet Muhammad. These narrations have been carefully collected, examined for authenticity, and classified accordingly. The two most authentic collections of Hadith are Sahih al-Bukhari and Sahih Muslim.

Five Pillars of Islam

1. Shahada (Declaration of Faith):
The Shahada is the fundamental declaration of Islamic belief, stating, "There is no god but Allah, and Muhammad is His Messenger." It affirms the oneness of Allah and the prophethood of Prophet Muhammad (peace be upon him).

2. Salat/Namaz (Prayer):
Muslims perform five daily prayers facing the Kaaba in Mecca. These prayers are observed at specific times:
1. Fajr (pre-dawn): 2 obligatory out of 4 rakat,
2. Dhuhr (midday): 4 obligatory out of 12 rakat,
3. Asr (late afternoon): 4 obligatory out of 8 rakat,
4. Maghrib (sunset): 3 obligatory out of 7 rakat,
5. Isha (night): 4 obligatory out of 17 rakat.

Prayer helps maintain a direct connection with Allah.

3. Zakat (Charity):
Zakat involves giving a portion of one's wealth to those in need, typically 2.5% of savings, given annually at the end of the year. It purifies wealth and provides support for the less fortunate in the community.

4. Sawm/Roza (Fasting during Ramadan):
During Ramadan, Muslims fast from dawn to sunset, abstaining from food, drink, and other physical needs. Fasting is a time for spiritual reflection, self-discipline, and increased devotion.

5. Hajj (Pilgrimage to Mecca):
Hajj is the pilgrimage to Mecca, required once in a lifetime for every Muslim who is physically and financially able. It takes place during the Islamic month of Dhu al-Hijjah and involves various rituals symbolizing unity and submission to Allah.

Six Articles of Faith

1. The belief in Allah (Tawhid):
This fundamental belief in the oneness of Allah encompasses His attributes of mercy, power, and wisdom. It affirms that Allah alone is the Creator and Sustainer of the universe.

2. The belief in angels (Mala'ika/Farishtey):
Angels are unseen beings created from light, tasked with carrying out Allah's commands, such as delivering revelations and recording human deeds. In Islam, the four main angels and their duties are:
(1) Jibril AS (Gabriel): Delivers Allah's revelations to prophets. (2) Mikail AS (Michael): Manages sustenance, rain, and natural events. (3) Israfil AS: Will blow the trumpet to signal the Day of Judgment. (4) Malik AS (Malak al Mawt): Takes the souls of the deceased.

3. The belief in the holy books (Kutub/Kitab):
Allah's guidance is preserved in divine scriptures, including the Tawrat (Torah), Zabur (Psalms), Injil (Gospel), and the Qur'an. However, the Qur'an is the final and unaltered revelation.

4. The belief in the prophets (Nabi and Rasul):
Prophets, from Adam (AS) to Muhammad (peace be upon him), were chosen to guide humanity. Each prophet conveyed divine messages to their respective communities, culminating in Prophet Muhammad's final revelation.

5. The belief in the Day of Judgment (Yawm al-Qiyamah):
On this day, all souls will be resurrected and held accountable for their deeds. This belief inspires Muslims to live righteously and uphold justice.

6. The belief in divine decree (Qadar):
Everything occurs by Allah's will, encompassing both favorable and challenging aspects of life. This belief instills trust and patience, recognizing Allah's supreme knowledge and wisdom.

Important Islamic Figures

Prophets/Anbiya

In the Qur'an, Allah has revealed the names of specific prophets who were sent as messengers to guide humanity toward righteousness and the worship of the One True God. While the exact number of prophets and messengers is known only to Allah, the Qur'an explicitly mentions 25 prophets by name, including Prophet Muhammad (peace be upon him). These prophets played pivotal roles in conveying Allah's message, demonstrating unwavering faith, and guiding their communities. The stories of these revered prophets highlight their contributions and the lessons they imparted. Each prophet serves as an exemplar of piety, patience, and obedience to Allah.

1. Prophet Adam AS: Mentioned 25 times in the Qur'an, Adam (AS) was created by Allah from clay, and life was breathed into him. The angels were commanded to prostrate before him, but Iblis refused and was cast out of Paradise. Adam (AS) and his wife, Hawwa (Eve), lived in Paradise until Iblis deceived them into eating from the forbidden tree, leading to their expulsion to Earth. As the father of humankind and the first prophet, Adam (AS) received divine guidance and taught his children about worship and obedience to Allah.

2. Prophet Idris AS (Enoch): Mentioned twice in the Qur'an, Idris (AS) was a truthful prophet who called people back to the religion of Adam (AS). He was born in Babylon and was known for his devotion and righteousness. Allah praised him and elevated him to a high status, as mentioned in Surah Maryam (19:56-57): "And mention Idris in the Book. Indeed, he was a man of truth and a prophet. And We raised him to a high position."

3. Prophet Nuh AS (Noah): Mentioned 43 times in the Qur'an, Nuh (AS) was sent to warn his people of a painful punishment if they did not worship Allah alone. He preached for 950 years, but most of his people rejected his message and persisted in their disbelief. Allah commanded Nuh (AS) to build an ark, and when the flood came, he and the believers were saved, while the disbelievers were drowned. His story exemplifies patience, perseverance, and trust in Allah's command.

4. Prophet Hud AS: Mentioned seven times in the Qur'an, Hud (AS) was sent to the people of 'Ad, a nation known for their strength and towering constructions. He called them to worship Allah alone, but they rejected his message. As a consequence of their arrogance and disbelief, they were destroyed by a violent storm as a divine punishment.

5. Prophet Salih AS: Mentioned nine times in the Qur'an, Salih (AS) was sent to the people of Thamud, urging them to worship Allah. As a sign of his truthfulness, he presented the miracle of a she-camel emerging from a rock. Despite witnessing this miracle, his people defied Allah's command by killing the camel, leading to their destruction through a devastating earthquake.

6. Prophet Ibrahim AS (Abraham): Mentioned 69 times in the Qur'an, Ibrahim (AS) called his people to monotheism, rejecting idol worship. Recognized as the forefather of many prophets, he was tested by Allah through numerous trials, including the command to sacrifice his son Isma'il (AS), which he faithfully accepted. He and Isma'il (AS) later built the Kaaba in Makkah, making him a central figure in Islamic faith and devotion.

7. Prophet Lut AS (Lot): Mentioned 27 times in the Qur'an, Lut (AS) was sent to the people of Sodom, warning them against their corrupt and immoral practices. Despite his persistent efforts, they refused to repent, leading to their total destruction through a divine punishment, while Lut (AS) and his believing family were saved.

8. Prophet Isma'il AS (Ishmael): Mentioned 12 times in the Qur'an, Isma'il (AS), the son of Ibrahim (AS), was known for his patience, obedience, and faithfulness. He assisted his father in constructing the Kaaba and was blessed with prophethood, calling people to worship Allah.

9. Prophet Ishaq (AS) (Isaac): Mentioned 16 times in the Qur'an, Ishaq (AS), the son of Ibrahim (AS), was granted prophethood and continued the message of monotheism. He was known for his righteousness and played a significant role in the lineage of prophets.

10. Prophet Ya'qub (AS) (Jacob): Mentioned 16 times in the Qur'an, Ya'qub (AS), the son of Ishaq (AS), was steadfast in his faith and trust in Allah. His story is closely linked to that of his son Yusuf (AS). He endured hardships with patience and remained devoted to Allah throughout his life.

10. Prophet Yusuf AS (Joseph): Mentioned 27 times in the Qur'an, Yusuf (AS) endured numerous trials, including the jealousy of his brothers, being thrown into a well, and imprisonment. Despite these hardships, he remained steadfast and ultimately rose to a position of authority in Egypt. His story, detailed in the Qur'an, is described as one of the best narratives, highlighting themes of patience, faith, and divine wisdom.

12. Prophet Shu'aib AS (Jethro): Mentioned 11 times in the Qur'an, Shu'aib (AS) was sent to the people of Madyan, calling them to worship Allah and practice honesty in trade. His people were known for their fraudulent business practices and corruption. They rejected his message, leading to their destruction by a severe earthquake as a divine punishment.

13. Prophet Ayyub AS (Job): Mentioned four times in the Qur'an, Ayyub (AS) is renowned for his unwavering patience and faith in the face of extreme suffering. He endured the loss of his wealth, health, and family but remained devoted to Allah. Eventually, Allah relieved his afflictions, restoring his health and blessings as a reward for his perseverance.

14. Prophet Dhul-Kifl AS: Mentioned twice in the Qur'an, Dhul-Kifl (AS) was known for his patience, righteousness, and dedication to fulfilling his commitments. Though little is detailed about his life, he is mentioned alongside other steadfast and virtuous prophets.

15. Prophet Musa AS (Moses): Mentioned 136 times in the Qur'an, Musa (AS) received revelation from Allah on Mount Sinai and was commanded to confront Pharaoh. With Allah's help, he performed miracles, including his staff turning into a snake, and led the Children of Israel out of Egypt. He was granted the Torah as guidance for his people and is among the most frequently mentioned prophets in the Qur'an, symbolizing leadership, faith, and resilience.

16. Prophet Harun AS (Aaron):
Mentioned 20 times in the Qur'an, Harun (AS) was the brother of Musa (AS) and was appointed as a prophet to assist him in delivering Allah's message to Pharaoh. He played a crucial role in guiding the Israelites and maintaining their faith during Musa's absence.

17. Prophet Dawud AS (David):
Mentioned 16 times in the Qur'an, Dawud (AS) was both a king and a prophet who received the Zabur (Psalms). He was known for his wisdom, justice, and exceptional skill in warfare. His devotion to Allah and his ability to rule with fairness made him a distinguished leader.

18. Prophet Sulaiman AS (Solomon):
Mentioned 17 times in the Qur'an, Sulaiman (AS) was a king and prophet blessed with immense wisdom and the unique ability to communicate with animals and jinn. He ruled with justice and undertook grand projects, including the construction of magnificent structures like the Temple of Solomon.

19. Prophet Ilyas AS (Elijah):
Mentioned three times in the Qur'an, Ilyas (AS) called his people to worship Allah alone and warned them against idolatry. Despite facing persecution, he remained steadfast in his faith and commitment to guiding his people.

20. Prophet Al-Yasa' AS (Elisha):
Mentioned twice in the Qur'an, Al-Yasa' (AS) continued the mission of Ilyas (AS) and was known for his righteousness. He was granted prophethood and is praised among the righteous servants of Allah.

21. Prophet Yunus AS (Jonah):
Mentioned four times in the Qur'an, Yunus (AS) initially left his people in frustration, but after being swallowed by a great fish, he repented and glorified Allah from within its belly. Upon his release, he returned to his people, who then accepted his message and repented.

22. Prophet Zakariyya AS (Zechariah): Mentioned seven times in the Qur'an, Zakariyya (AS) was known for his devotion and piety. He prayed earnestly for a son, and Allah granted him Yahya (AS), a righteous and noble prophet.

23. Prophet Yahya AS (John): Mentioned five times in the Qur'an, Yahya (AS) was a prophet known for his wisdom, piety, and righteousness from a young age. He was given divine scripture and remained steadfast in his faith.

24. Prophet 'Isa AS (Jesus): Mentioned 25 times in the Qur'an, 'Isa (AS) is described as the son of Mary, born without a father as a miraculous sign from Allah. He was a messenger who performed miracles by Allah's permission and called people to worship the One True God. The Qur'an emphasizes that he was not the son of God, refuting Christian beliefs about his divinity.

Companions/Sahaba

The Companions of Prophet Muhammad (peace be upon him), known as the Sahaba, were those who met him during his lifetime, believed in his message, and embraced Islam. Their unwavering faith and dedication played a crucial role in spreading Islam and preserving its teachings.

These Companions participated in significant events, including battles, and were instrumental in transmitting the Qur'an and Hadith. Their lives offer invaluable lessons. Below are the struggles and achievements of 18 of these distinguished individuals.

Abu Bakr As-Siddeeq (RA)

Known as As-Siddeeq (the most truthful) and Al-'Ateeq (the one liberated from Hellfire), Abu Bakr (RA) was the first Caliph of Islam.

- <u>Struggles</u>: Faced widespread apostasy after the Prophet's passing, led military campaigns against rebels, including Musailimah the Liar, and initially hesitated to compile the Qur'an but was later convinced by 'Umar (RA).
- <u>Achievements</u>: Suppressed apostasy movements, commissioned the compilation of the Qur'an by Zaid bin Thabit (RA), devoted his life to Islam, supported the poor, and donated all his possessions for the Tabuk Expedition.

'Umar bin Al-Khattab (RA)

The second Caliph of Islam, also known as Al-Faruq (the Distinguisher between right and wrong).

- <u>Struggles</u>: Initially a fierce opponent of Islam, later faced administrative challenges in governing an expanding empire and was assassinated while leading prayers.
- <u>Achievements</u>: Implemented strong governance, oversaw major conquests in Iraq, Syria, and Egypt, ensured justice and welfare for the people, and appointed a council of six Companions to select his successor.

'Uthman bin 'Affan (RA)

The third Caliph of Islam, known as "Possessor of Two Lights."

- <u>Struggles</u>: Faced disputes over variations in Qur'anic recitation, dealt with rebellion and false accusations, and was ultimately assassinated.
- <u>Achievements</u>: Standardized the Qur'an in the Quraishi dialect and distributed copies to major regions, preventing discrepancies. Known for his generosity, modesty, and unwavering adherence to Islamic principles.

'Ali bin Abi Talib (RA)

The fourth Caliph of Islam, also called "The Lion of Allah."

- <u>Struggles</u>: His caliphate was marked by internal strife and opposition from various factions, ultimately leading to his assassination.
- <u>Achievements</u>: The first young boy to embrace Islam, married Fatimah (RA), renowned for his bravery and heroism, served as a distinguished judge, and led a simple, ascetic life.

'Abdullah bin 'Umar (RA)

A prominent scholar and jurist.

- <u>Struggles</u>: Eager to support the Prophet (peace be upon him) in spreading Islam from a young age, but his father, 'Umar (RA), refrained from assigning him official responsibilities. Despite being urged to include him in the council to select the next Caliph, 'Umar (RA) declined. 'Uthman (RA) later offered him a judicial position, which he also rejected.
- <u>Achievements</u>: A devout follower of Islam, deeply attached to Allah and the Prophet (peace be upon him). Guided by the Prophet and his father, he became a renowned scholar who strictly adhered to the Qur'an and Sunnah. Though he held no formal office, his father frequently consulted him on matters of Islamic governance. He advised Caliph 'Uthman (RA) and remained loyal to him despite rejecting an official judicial role.

Abu Dhar Al-Gifari (RA)

Advocate of Equality and Justice.

- <u>Struggles</u>: Faced severe oppression and persecution for being among the early converts to Islam. Known for his outspoken nature and strong opposition to the accumulation of wealth.
- <u>Achievements</u>: A devout follower of the Prophet (peace be upon him), he dedicated his life to supporting the poor and needy. Renowned for his humility and simplicity, he was praised by the Prophet, who said, "May Allah have mercy on Abu Dhar, for he marches alone, dies alone, and will be resurrected alone."

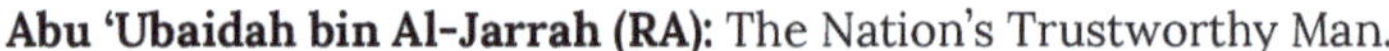

Abu 'Ubaidah bin Al-Jarrah (RA): The Nation's Trustworthy Man.
- <u>Struggles</u>: Endured early oppression and torture in Makkah alongside other early Muslims. Migrated to Abyssinia to escape persecution. Later faced challenges from the Quraysh's continued aggression after migrating to Madinah, including hardships in the Battle of Uhud.
- <u>Achievements</u>: Among the earliest converts to Islam, he migrated to Madinah and contributed to the establishment of the Islamic state. Led an unarmed faction of the Muslim army that peacefully entered Makkah during its conquest. Appointed by the Prophet as the treasurer of the emerging Islamic state. Played a vital role in military campaigns, leading the Muslim army at the Battle of Yarmouk against the Romans. Participated in the conquest of Syria and was entrusted with key leadership roles, demonstrating his integrity and trustworthiness.

'Amr bin Al-'Aas (RA): The Conqueror of Egypt.
- <u>Struggles</u>: Initially opposed Islam but later embraced it and became a pivotal figure in the early Muslim community.
- <u>Achievements</u>: Known for his intelligence and strategic thinking, he played a significant role in shaping the history of Islam. Most notably, he led the conquest of Egypt and established Al-Fustat as its administrative center. Served as Egypt's governor during the Caliphates of 'Umar and 'Uthman (RA), utilizing his political acumen to strengthen Egypt as a key support for other Muslim territories. Recognized as a daring, resolute, and skillful statesman, admired for his wisdom and strategic leadership.

Az-Zubair bin Al-Awwam (RA)
The Disciple.
- <u>Struggles</u>: Faced early persecution for accepting Islam and endured hardships in his dedication to the faith. Participated in numerous significant battles.
- <u>Achievements</u>: Played a crucial role in suppressing apostate rebellions after the Prophet's passing. Selected by 'Umar (RA) as one of the six candidates for the Caliphate. Remained committed to Islam during 'Uthman's (RA) rule and actively participated in military campaigns. Carried the Prophet's flag during the conquest of Makkah, symbolizing his loyalty and leadership.

Bilal bin Rabah (RA)
The Mu'adhdhin (Caller to Prayer).
- <u>Struggles</u>: Born into slavery and endured brutal torture at the hands of his master for embracing Islam.
- <u>Achievements</u>: Known for his unwavering faith, he became the first and most honored Mu'adhdhin of Islam. His resilience and devotion made him a symbol of endurance, and he overcame oppression to become a respected figure in the Muslim community.

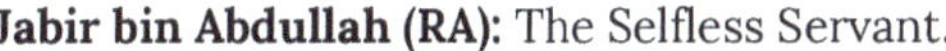

Jabir bin Abdullah (RA): The Selfless Servant.
- <u>Struggles</u>: Endured hardships and challenges during the early days of Islam.
- <u>Achievements</u>: Demonstrated exceptional dedication and sacrifice, participating in numerous battles alongside the Prophet (peace be upon him). As a key narrator of Ahadith, he contributed significantly to preserving and transmitting the Prophet's teachings.

Khabbab bin Al-Aratt (RA): The Teacher.
- <u>Struggles</u>: Faced severe torture for his faith but remained steadfast and actively invited others to Islam.
- <u>Achievements</u>: One of the few Arabs proficient in reading and writing during that time, he played a crucial role in teaching the Qur'an to early Muslims. His efforts in educating others helped strengthen the Muslim community's understanding of their faith.

Khalid bin Al-Waleed (RA)

The Sword of Allah.
- <u>Struggles</u>: Initially opposed Islam but later embraced it, becoming one of its most formidable commanders.
- <u>Achievements</u>: Renowned for his unmatched military strategy and leadership, he led the Muslim army to victory in numerous crucial battles. Despite being dismissed from his command by Caliph 'Umar (RA), he humbly accepted the decision and continued fighting as an ordinary soldier. His contributions were instrumental in the rapid expansion and consolidation of the Islamic state.

Sa'd bin Abi Waqqas (RA)

The Lion in the Deen.
- <u>Struggles</u>: Faced opposition from his family for accepting Islam and endured hardships in his commitment to the faith. Supported Abu Bakr (RA) in suppressing the apostasy movements after the Prophet's death.
- <u>Achievements</u>: A fearless warrior known for his devotion to restoring peace and preventing a return to idolatry. Played a significant role in the early military campaigns that strengthened the Islamic state.

Sa'd bin Mu'adh (RA)

The True Supporter of Islam.
- <u>Struggles</u>: Encountered opposition and challenges in the early days of Islam.
- <u>Achievements</u>: A staunch supporter of the Prophet Muhammad (peace be upon him) and a key figure in the Muslim community. His leadership was crucial during the Battle of the Trench. His death was deeply mourned, as it marked a great loss for the early Muslim community.

Salman Al-Farisi (RA): The Truth Seeker.

- <u>Struggles</u>: Born into Persian nobility, he embarked on a long and difficult journey in search of the true religion, facing numerous hardships before embracing Islam.
- <u>Achievements</u>: Known for his wisdom and innovative thinking, he suggested the trench strategy during the Battle of the Confederates, which played a decisive role in the Muslim victory. He participated in many battles and later served as a just and humble governor, displaying great compassion for the poor and needy.

Suhaib Ar-Roomi (RA)

The Selfless Servant

- <u>Struggles</u>: Enslaved as a child but later gained his freedom. Faced a difficult choice between his wealth and his faith.
- <u>Achievements</u>: Demonstrated immense sacrifice by choosing his faith over material wealth. Praised by the Prophet (peace be upon him) for his devotion. Known for his mercy and generosity, particularly towards orphans and the needy. Earned the trust of Caliph 'Umar (RA), who appointed him to lead the Muslims in prayer after being fatally wounded.

Talhah bin 'Ubaidullah (RA)

The Living Martyr

- <u>Struggles</u>: Endured persecution for embracing Islam early on and actively participated in several battles.
- <u>Achievements</u>: Provided financial support to the Muslim community and dedicated his life to the cause of Islam. Renowned for his bravery and recognized by the Prophet (peace be upon him) as a potential martyr. Played a crucial role in urging 'Ali (RA) to accept the Caliphate after the assassination of 'Uthman (RA).

Chapter 3

Rights and Duties

Parents

1. **Obedience and Respect**: Parents must be obeyed in all permissible matters, provided it does not lead to disobedience to Allah.

2. **Kindness and Good Treatment**: Show affection, care, and good conduct towards parents at all times.

3. **Lowering the Wing of Humility**: Display utmost humility and gentleness, especially as they grow older.

4. **Financial and Emotional Support**: Children are responsible for assisting their parents in times of need, ensuring their well-being and comfort.

5. **Earning Their Duas (Prayers)**: Strive to gain their pleasure and prayers, as they hold immense power and blessings.

6. **Prioritizing Parents After Allah and His Messenger**: Parents have the greatest right over their children after Allah and His Messenger (peace be upon him).

7. **Seeking Their Advice and Permission**: Value their wisdom, seek their guidance, and involve them in significant life decisions.

8. **Praying for Them (Alive and After Death)**: Continuously pray for their forgiveness, mercy, and well-being.

9. **Maintaining Family Ties on Their Behalf**: Honor their legacy by keeping strong ties with relatives and their close friends.

10. **Repaying Their Sacrifices**: Show gratitude for their sacrifices and strive to repay them, even though their efforts can never truly be repaid in full.

11. **Caring for Parents Above Others**: Prioritize their needs and service over optional acts of worship or other commitments.

12. **Forgiving and Being Patient with Them**: Show patience in times of difficulty, especially if they become demanding or difficult in old age.

13. **Avoiding Harsh Words or Actions**: Even minor expressions of annoyance, like "uff," are prohibited.

14. **Making Their Happiness a Priority**: Actively seek ways to bring joy and comfort to them.

15. **Showing Gratitude Even in Their Absence**: Acknowledge their contributions and remain grateful for their sacrifices.

16. **Honoring Their Promises**: Fulfill any promises or commitments they have left behind.

17. **Charity on Their Behalf**: Perform charitable acts in their name, such as Sadaqah Jariyah (ongoing charity).

18. **Being the Cause of Their Forgiveness**: Through good deeds and dua, strive to be a source of forgiveness for their shortcomings.

19. **Respecting Their Wishes**: Honor their preferences and desires when they are reasonable and halal.

20. **Maintaining Dignity and Honor**: Speak of your parents respectfully, protecting their honor and dignity in public and private.

Relatives

1. **Maintaining Ties of Kinship**: It is a fundamental duty to stay connected with relatives and nurture family bonds through visits, calls, or messages.

2. **Providing Financial Support**: Relatives in need have a right to financial assistance if one is capable of helping.

3. **Offering Emotional Support**: Show kindness, empathy, and emotional support to relatives, especially during times of hardship or joy.

4. **Respecting Elders**: Honor and respect elder relatives by valuing their wisdom and status in the family.

5. **Mentoring the Young**: Offer guidance, care, and love to younger relatives to support their growth and well-being.

6. **Sharing in Celebrations and Grief**: Take part in family events such as weddings, funerals, and other gatherings to strengthen relationships.

7. **Maintaining Justice and Fairness**: Treat all relatives fairly, avoiding favoritism or discrimination based on wealth, status, or other factors.

8. **Forgiving Mistakes**: Show patience and forgiveness when conflicts or misunderstandings arise within the family.

9. **Speaking Well of Relatives**: Protect their dignity by refraining from gossip or slander and speaking positively about them.

10. **Fulfilling Promises and Commitments**: Honor any promises or obligations made to relatives.

11. **Supporting During Hardships:** Assist relatives in times of illness, financial difficulty, or other challenges.

12. **Offering Advice and Guidance**: Provide thoughtful counsel and support to help them make beneficial decisions.

13. **Praying for Them**: Make dua for their guidance, success, and well-being in both this world and the hereafter.

14. **Giving Gifts**: Strengthen family bonds by occasionally giving gifts, no matter how small.

15. **Visiting and Checking on Them**: Maintain strong ties by visiting or checking in on relatives, especially those who live alone or far away.

16. **Avoiding Harsh Words or Actions**: Interact with gentleness and refrain from words or actions that could cause harm or distress.

17. **Cooperating in Goodness**: Encourage and assist relatives in engaging in good deeds while discouraging harmful or sinful actions.

18. **Making Dua for Their Reconciliation**: Pray for peace and resolution when conflicts arise among relatives.

19. **Providing Moral Support in Worship and Faith**: Encourage and support relatives in their religious practices, helping to strengthen their faith.

20. **Being Grateful for Their Role in Your Life**: Acknowledge and appreciate the positive impact they have had through their support, guidance, or care.

Neighbors

1. **Showing Patience and Tolerance**: Be patient and forgiving if a neighbor causes minor inconvenience or annoyance.

2. **Resolving Disputes Peacefully**: Handle disagreements with neighbors calmly and fairly, avoiding hostility or prolonged conflict.

3. **Offering Hospitality**: Welcome neighbors warmly into your home when appropriate, fostering a spirit of friendship.

4. **Being Respectful During Gatherings**: Keep noise levels and gatherings considerate, ensuring they do not disturb those living nearby.

5. **Assisting in Times of Emergency**: Offer immediate help if your neighbor faces an urgent situation, such as illness or an accident.

6. **Encouraging Good Conduct**: Promote mutual respect and encourage positive behavior within the neighborhood.

7. **Standing by Them in Difficult Times**: Support neighbors during personal losses or hardships, showing empathy and care.

8. **Teaching Children Neighborly Etiquette**: Instill in your family the importance of respecting and caring for neighbors.

9. **Keeping Public Spaces Clean**: Take responsibility for maintaining shared spaces like corridors, gardens, and streets.

10. **Being a Source of Positivity**: Foster a welcoming and friendly environment by spreading kindness, goodwill, and cooperation in the neighborhood.

11. **Forgiving Disputes**: Exercise patience and forgiveness in case of disagreements, prioritizing peace and harmony.

12. **Praying for Them**: Regularly include neighbors in prayers, seeking their well-being and success.

13. **Supporting Them in Times of Joy and Grief**: Share in their happiness during celebrations and offer condolences and assistance during times of loss.

14. **Guiding Them to Goodness**: Encourage neighbors towards beneficial actions and offer gentle advice against harmful behaviors when necessary.

15. **Not Blocking Their Path**: Keep shared spaces such as stairways, roads, or entrances clear to ensure ease of movement for everyone.

16. **Giving Them Preference**: Show selflessness by prioritizing their needs whenever possible.

17. **Encouraging Community Engagement**: Promote a supportive and united neighborhood through positive initiatives and participation.

18. **Treating Non-Muslim Neighbors with Justice**: Uphold fairness and integrity in all dealings, regardless of religious differences.

19. **Showing Kindness to Non-Muslim Neighbors**: Extend compassion and goodwill, embodying the principles of good character and ethical conduct.

20. **Maintaining Peaceful Relations with Non-Muslim Neighbors**: Foster a harmonious environment by avoiding conflict and being a source of understanding and peace.

Chapter 4

Morals from The Qur'an

1. Do not lie.
2. Do not spy.
3. Do not exult.
4. Do not insult.
5. Do not waste.
6. Feed the poor.
7. Do not backbite.
8. Keep your oaths.
9. Do not take bribes.
10. Honour your treaties.
11. Restrain your anger.
12. Do not spread gossip.
13. Think well of others.
14. Be good to guests.
15. Do not harm believers.
16. Do not be rude to parents.
17. Turn away from ill speech.
18. Do not make fun of others.
19. Walk in a humble manner.
20. Respond to evil with good.
21. Do not say what you do not do.
22. Keep your trusts and promises.
23. Do not insult others' false gods.
24. Do not deceive people in trade.
25. Do not take items without right.
26. Do not ask unnecessary questions.
27. Do not be miserly or extravagant.
28. Do not call others by bad names.
29. Do not claim yourselves to be pure.
30. Speak nicely, even to the ignorant.
31. Do not ask for repayment for favours.
32. Make room for others at gatherings.
33. If the enemy wants peace, then accept it.
34. Return a greeting in a better manner.
35. Do not remind others of your favours.

36. Make peace between fighting groups.

37. Lower your voice and talk moderately.

38. Don't let hatred cause you to be unjust.

39. Don't ask too many favours from people.

40. Greet people when entering their home.

41. Be just, even against yourself & relatives.

42. Speak gently, even to leaders of disbelief.

43. Don't criticize small contributions of others.

44. Don't call the Prophet how you call others.

45. Try to make peace between husband & wife.

46. Don't call the Prophet from outside his rooms.

47. Oppression/corruption is worse than killing.

48. Preach to others in a good and wise manner.

49. Don't accuse others of immorality without proof.

50. Consider wives of the Prophet like your mothers.

51. Don't raise your voice above that of the Prophet's.

52. Don't call someone a disbeliever without knowing.

53. Seek permission before entering someone's room.

54. Know your enemies can become your close friends.

55. Don't wrongly consume the wealth of the vulnerable.

56. Don't turn your cheek away from people in arrogance.

57. Forgive others, as you would like Allah to forgive you.

58. Seek Prophet's permission when leaving his gathering.

59. Don't hold secret meetings for sin, rather do so for piety.

60. Don't order others to do good while forgetting it yourself.

61. Be patient with your teacher & follow his instructions.

62. Don't frown, turn away or neglect those who come to you.

63. If unable to help a needy person, at least speak nice words.

64. Be lenient to those under you, and consult them in matters.

65. Verify information from a dubious source before acting upon it.

66. Don't remain in the Prophet's home unnecessarily after a meal.

67. Continue spending on those less fortunate.

68. Don't enter homes without permission & return if refused entry.

69. Avoid sitting with those who mock religion until they change the subject.

70. Say it's not appropriate to talk of slander when it's mentioned to you.

71. If required to ask the Prophet's wives, then do so from behind a screen.
72. Divorce in an amicable manner instead of keeping and harming your wife.
73. Punish in an equivalent manner to how you were harmed, or be patient.
74. Differences in color and language are signs of Allah, not means of superiority.
75. Do not take women by force, nor take back the bridal gift without a valid reason, and live with them in kindness.

The Qur'an provides a comprehensive ethical framework that guides individuals toward righteousness, justice, and compassion. It emphasizes values such as honesty, patience, kindness, humility, and the importance of fulfilling responsibilities toward family, society, and even strangers. The teachings encourage self-discipline, gratitude, forgiveness, and generosity while warning against arrogance, dishonesty, and oppression.

Moreover, the Qur'an promotes balance in all aspects of life—spiritual, social, and personal—ensuring that morality is not just theoretical but practical and applicable to daily living. These moral principles are not limited or bound by time; rather, they serve as an ever-relevant source of guidance, adaptable to various circumstances while maintaining their core essence of justice and goodness. Ultimately, the Qur'an teaches that true success lies in sincerity, faith, and righteous conduct, benefiting both the individual and society as a whole.

Misconceptions

Misconceptions and Their Quranic Context

1. Misconception: Islam prescribes extreme punishments without mercy.
   - Context: **Punishments such as for theft or adultery have strict conditions and serve as deterrents rather than arbitrary punishments. Islam emphasizes repentance, forgiveness, and social justice before enforcing penalties (Qur'an 5:38-39, 24:2). Many punishments are waived if the accused repents or if doubt exists.**
   - Reference: Qur'an 5:38-39, 24:2

2. Misconception: Islam commands Muslims to attack and kill non-Muslims.
   - Context: **Fighting is permitted only in self-defense against oppression or aggression. Islam strictly forbids harming civilians, destroying property, or breaking peace agreements. If the enemy seeks peace, Muslims must accept it (Qur'an 2:190-193, 8:60-61).**
   - Reference: Qur'an 2:190-193, 8:60-61

3. Misconception: Muslim men can marry as many wives as they want, while polyandry is unfairly prohibited.
   - Context: **Islam restricts polygamy to a maximum of four wives and only if justice can be maintained; otherwise, monogamy is required (Qur'an 4:3, 4:129). Historically, this protected widows and orphans rather than granting privilege to men.**
   - Why Polyandry Is Prohibited: **Islam forbids polyandry due to complications in lineage, inheritance, and family stability. Unclear paternity could lead to disputes over rights, responsibilities, and genetic identity, whereas polygyny does not create such issues (Qur'an 4:23, 33:4-5).**
   - Reference: Qur'an 4:3, 4:129, 4:23, 33:4-5

4. Misconception: The Qur'an teaches that the Earth is flat.
Context: **The Qur'an describes the Earth's shape in alignment with its spherical nature, referencing its rotation, orbit, and the alternation of day and night (Qur'an 79:30, 21:33, 36:40). Early Muslim scholars contributed significantly to astronomy, proving Islam aligns with scientific discoveries.**
  - Reference: Qur'an 79:30, 21:33, 36:40

5. Misconception: Jihad is about violent war to spread Islam.
  - Context: **Jihad primarily refers to striving for righteousness, self-improvement, and social justice. Armed struggle is only allowed in self-defense or to protect religious freedom (Qur'an 22:39-40). Forced conversion is strictly forbidden (Qur'an 2:256, 10:99).**
  - Reference: Qur'an 22:39-40, 2:256, 10:99

6. Misconception: Islam treats women as inferior and forces them into strict dress codes.
  - Context: **Islam grants women equal spiritual and moral status to men (Qur'an 33:35) while recognizing their distinct roles. Women have the right to education, own and inherit property (Qur'an 4:7), financial independence (Qur'an 4:32), and protection from harm. Islam prohibits forced marriage, grants women the right to accept or reject proposals (Qur'an 4:19), and allows them to seek divorce. The responsibility of financial support lies with men, ensuring women's security. Islam honors mothers, with the Prophet Muhammad (peace be upon him) stating that paradise lies beneath a mother's feet. Any form of abuse or mistreatment of women is against Islamic teachings. Surah An-Nisa (The Women) is dedicated to women's rights. Regarding the hijab, Islam mandates modest dress for women (Qur'an 24:31) but does not permit coercion. While failing to observe hijab may be sinful, forcing it contradicts Islamic principles. Likewise, men must lower their gaze and maintain modesty (Qur'an 24:30). Both are accountable for their obligations, and failing to uphold them is considered sinful.**
  - Reference: Qur'an 33:35, 4:7, 4:19, 4:32, 2:228, 24:30-31

Islamic teachings are often misunderstood due to selective quoting and lack of context. A deeper look into the Qur'an and Hadith shows that Islam upholds justice, peace, and morality. These points offer a brief clarification, but for a full understanding, one should read the Qur'an and Hadith.

Conclusion

In conclusion, Nur of Truth offers a well-rounded guide to understanding the core principles of Islam. It explores the Foundations of Islam by detailing the essence of the faith, the attributes of Allah, the significance of Prophet Muhammad (PBUH), and the importance of the Qur'an and Sunnah. It also thoroughly explains the Five Pillars of Islam and the Six Articles of Faith, which form the bedrock of Islamic beliefs and practices.

It introduces Important Islamic Figures, shedding light on the roles and teachings of the Prophets and the Companions (Sahaba) of Prophet Muhammad (PBUH), who provide timeless lessons through their dedication and actions.

It outlines Rights and Duties, focusing on the obligations Muslims have towards their parents, relatives, and neighbors, and highlighting the significance of fostering supportive and respectful relationships within the community.

It delves into Morals from the Qur'an, offering ethical guidance rooted in divine teachings. This section underscores the Qur'an's role as a source of moral and spiritual wisdom, guiding individuals toward a just and upright life.

Additionally, it addresses common misconceptions about Islam, clarifying misunderstandings related to justice in Islamic law, the true meaning of jihad, women's rights, and other frequently misinterpreted topics. By providing context and explanation, it highlights Islam's emphasis on peace, justice, and moral integrity.

Overall, Nur of Truth emphasizes the holistic nature of Islam, encouraging spiritual growth, moral integrity, and community unity based on divine principles, the teachings of Prophet Muhammad (PBUH), and the exemplary lives of revered figures in Islamic history.

References

The content in "Nur of Truth" is meticulously compiled from a variety of authentic Islamic sources and scholarly works.

The primary sources among many others include the Qur'an, which is the central religious text of Islam considered by Muslims to be the literal word of Allah as revealed to Prophet Muhammad (peace be upon him); Hadith, which are collections of the sayings, actions, and approvals of Prophet Muhammad (peace be upon him) that provide guidance on various aspects of life; Stories of the Prophets, which recount the lives and missions of the Prophets and emphasize their role in conveying Allah's message; The Golden Series of the Prophet's Companions, which highlights the lives, contributions, and exemplary conduct of the Companions (Sahaba) of Prophet Muhammad (peace be upon him); and other scholarly insights from renowned Islamic scholars who offer in-depth analysis and commentary on Islamic teachings and practices.

Special thanks are extended to all the scholars and sources whose invaluable contributions have made this compilation possible. Their dedication to preserving and sharing Islamic knowledge continues to guide and inspire.

Additional Reading (Stories)

The Merchant's Honor

In the grand bazaar of Damascus, Kareem was known for his honesty. Unlike others, he never lied, deceived in trade, or took bribes. His shop flourished because customers trusted him.

One day, a wealthy trader offered him a fortune to sell low-quality silk as premium fabric. Kareem refused. "Wealth without honor is a curse," he said. The trader scoffed and left.

Later, a poor man approached Kareem. "I have only a few coins. Will you sell me good fabric for my daughter's wedding?"

Kareem nodded and gave him the finest silk at cost price. "A daughter's joy is worth more than profit," he said.

Soon, an ambassador sought a merchant to supply goods for a royal treaty. Kareem was chosen for his reputation of keeping promises and fairness. His competitors, who had mocked him, now envied him.

One day, a dishonest merchant was caught and punished for bribery. Kareem's just dealings had protected him from such disgrace. When his son asked why he refused easy wealth, Kareem said, "Walk humbly, speak kindly, and never betray trust—honor is the greatest currency."

Morals Learned:
- Don't lie. (Kareem refused to deceive his customers.)
- Don't take bribes. (He did not accept money for dishonest trade.)
- Honor your treaties. (He was chosen for a royal contract due to honesty.)
- Keep your trusts and promises. (He ensured fair trade and kept his word.)
- Don't deceive people in trade. (He sold only quality fabric at fair prices.)
- Don't take items without right. (He refused to overcharge the poor man.)
- Don't be miserly nor extravagant. (He balanced fair profit with generosity.)
- Speak nicely, even to the ignorant. (He remained polite to mocking traders.)
- Walk in a humble manner. (Despite his success, he remained grounded.)
- Be just, even against yourself and relatives. (He never let greed corrupt him.)

The Silent Lesson

Master Idris, a wise teacher, never insulted, spread gossip, or exulted over others' failures. He taught by example, speaking only when necessary.

One day, a student named Rashid spread lies about him, hoping to ruin his reputation. Idris neither defended himself nor sought revenge. Instead, he continued to teach with patience and kindness.

Rashid's slander spread, but Idris remained calm. A villager mocked, "Why do you let a mere boy ruin your name?"

Idris replied, "Hatred poisons the heart, but patience purifies the soul."

Days later, Rashid expected retaliation but saw Idris helping the poor and responding to rude people with wisdom. Confused, he asked, "Why don't you expose me?"

Idris smiled. "If I respond to evil with evil, I booome like you." Rashid, ashamed, confessed his wrongdoing before the class. From that day on, he became Idris's most devoted student.

The class learned a powerful lesson: true wisdom lies in patience, dignity, and choosing kindness even when wronged.

Morals Learned:
- Don't exult. (Idris never rejoiced at others' failures.)
- Don't insult. (He never responded with harsh words.)
- Restrain your anger. (He remained calm despite slander.)
- Don't spread gossip. (He refused to engage in rumors.)
- Turn away from ill speech. (He ignored harmful talk.)
- Respond to evil with good. (He forgave Rashid instead of punishing him.)
- Don't call others with bad names. (He never insulted Rashid.)
- Don't remind others of your favors. (He helped the poor without boasting.)
- Don't let hatred cause you to be unjust. (He refused to seek revenge.)
- Forgive others as you would like Allah to forgive you. (He forgave Rashid.)

The Stranger's Greeting

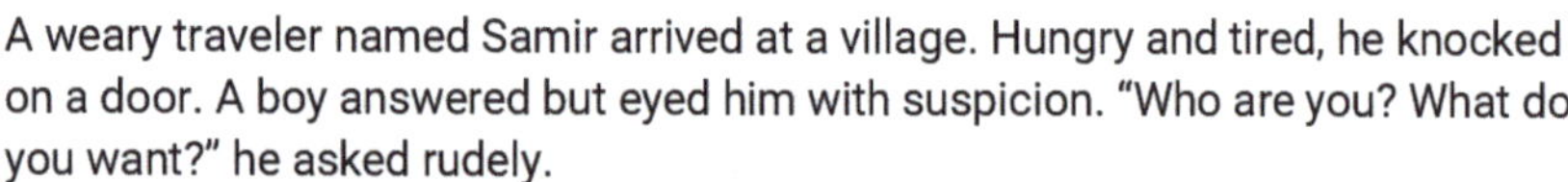

A weary traveler named Samir arrived at a village. Hungry and tired, he knocked on a door. A boy answered but eyed him with suspicion. "Who are you? What do you want?" he asked rudely.

Samir smiled. "Peace be upon you," he said gently. "May I have a drink of water?"

The boy hesitated but gave him a small cup. Samir thanked him warmly and walked away humbly. Curious, the boy followed him and saw him greet strangers with kindness, never turning his cheek away in arrogance.

At the village square, an elder suddenly rushed to embrace Samir. "You saved my life years ago," he revealed.

The boy, ashamed of his rudeness, hurried home. That night, he told his father, "I misjudged a man by his appearance, but his manners proved his worth." His father nodded, saying, "Remember, son, character is seen in how we treat strangers, not in their looks."

Morals Learned:
- Don't waste. (The traveler was content with a simple drink.)
- Be good to guests. (The boy eventually learned to treat guests kindly.)
- Walk in a humble manner. (Samir walked away humbly instead of reacting.)
- Don't ask unnecessary questions. (The boy learned not to interrogate rudely.)
- Make room for others at gatherings. (Samir greeted all warmly.)
- Return a greeting in a better manner. (Samir showed kindness despite rudeness.)
- Greet people when entering their home. (He greeted the boy before asking for help.)
- Don't turn your cheek away from people in arrogance. (He treated all equally.)
- Say it's not appropriate to discuss slander when it is mentioned to you. (The boy learned to avoid gossip.)
- Know that enemies can become close friends. (He changed the boy's heart through kindness.)

The King's Test

King Idris was known for his wisdom and justice. One day, two men came before him with a dispute. One accused the other of stealing, while the accused man swore he was innocent.

The king turned to his advisors. "Verify information from dubious sources before acting," he instructed. Upon investigation, they discovered the accuser had lied out of jealousy.

Later, a noble offered Idris a bribe to favor him in a land dispute. Idris refused, saying, "Justice is not for sale." The noble grew angry and insulted the king.

Yet, Idris remained calm. "Lower your voice and talk moderately," he advised. "Hatred must not lead to injustice."

The noble, embarrassed, sought forgiveness. Idris accepted and ensured peace between the two rivals.

That night, he told his son, "A ruler must be just, patient, and never let greed or anger cloud his judgment."

Morals Learned:
- Don't take bribes. (Idris refused to be swayed by wealth.)
- Be just, even against yourself and relatives. (He judged fairly despite noble influence.)
- Verify information from dubious sources before acting upon it. (He investigated before passing judgment.)
- Don't insult others' false gods. (He refused to mock the noble's beliefs.)
- Don't deceive people in trade. (The false accuser's lie was exposed.)
- Don't let hatred cause you to be unjust. (Idris remained fair despite insults.)
- Lower your voice and talk moderately. (He spoke calmly to the angry noble.)
- Make peace between fighting groups. (He settled the dispute peacefully.)
- Punish in a manner equivalent to how you were harmed, or exercise patience. (He chose patience over punishment.)
- Preach to others in a good and wise manner. (He advised his son wisely.)

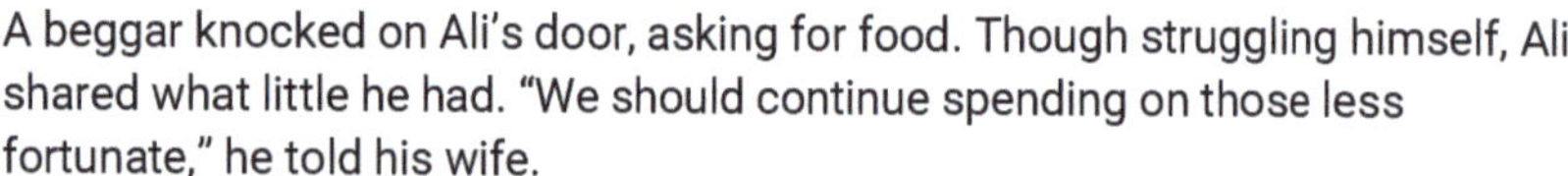

The Unseen Reward

A beggar knocked on Ali's door, asking for food. Though struggling himself, Ali shared what little he had. "We should continue spending on those less fortunate," he told his wife.

That night, he saw his neighbor mistreating his servant. He intervened, saying, "Live with kindness, not cruelty."

One day, a man criticized Ali for his small acts of charity. "What use are a few coins?" the man mocked.

Ali smiled. "No kindness is too small."

Later, Ali found a bag of gold outside his home. A note read: "Your goodness has returned to you." He never knew who left it, but he knew kindness always comes back in unseen ways.

Morals Learned:
- Feed the poor. (Ali gave food despite his own struggles.)
- Continue spending on those less fortunate. (He believed in charity despite poverty.)
- Don't criticize small contributions of others. (He defended small acts of kindness.)
- Be lenient with those under you. (He encouraged kindness toward servants.)
- Live with women in kindness. (He advised his neighbor to be just.)
- Don't remain in the Prophet's home unnecessarily after a meal. (He respected privacy and time.)
- Seek permission before entering someone's room. (He knocked before helping the servant.)
- If unable to help a needy person, at least speak kind words. (He always spoke kindly.)
- Return a greeting in a better manner. (He responded warmly even to critics.)
- Oppression or corruption is worse than killing. (He opposed mistreatment of the servant.)

The Two Travelers

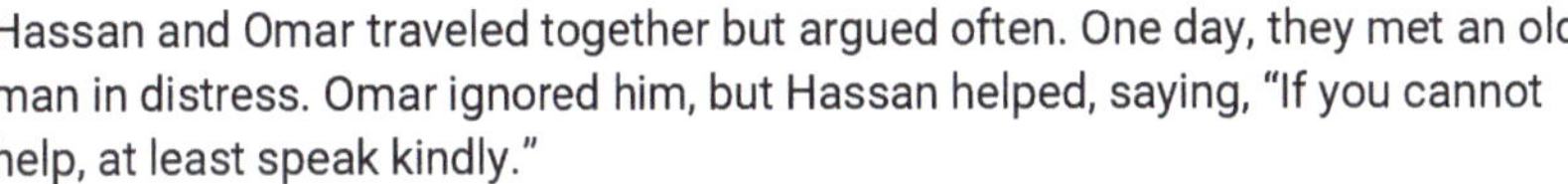

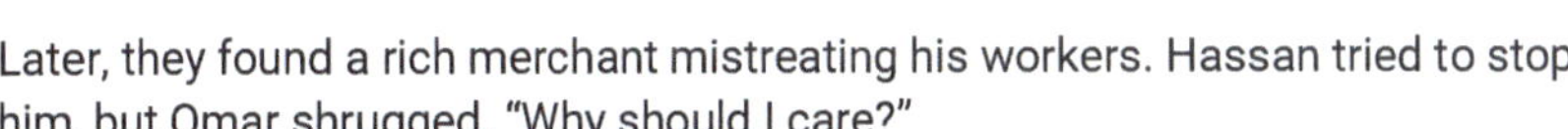

Hassan and Omar traveled together but argued often. One day, they met an old man in distress. Omar ignored him, but Hassan helped, saying, "If you cannot help, at least speak kindly."

Later, they found a rich merchant mistreating his workers. Hassan tried to stop him, but Omar shrugged. "Why should I care?"

At night, they camped under the stars. "Why do you always interfere?" Omar asked.

Hassan replied, "Because no man is superior to another, except by kindness."

The next morning, the merchant found them and apologized. "Your words made me reflect."

Omar finally understood: small acts of goodness create ripples that change the world.

Morals Learned:
- If unable to help a needy person, at least speak kind words. (Hassan helped the old man.)
- Don't ask too many favors from people. (He never expected anything in return.)
- Differences in color and language are signs of Allah, not means of superiority. (He treated all equally.)
- Know that enemies can become close friends. (The merchant changed his ways.)
- Don't ask unnecessary questions. (Hassan focused on doing good rather than debating.)
- Say it's not appropriate to discuss slander when it is mentioned to you. (He stopped unnecessary talk.)
- Greet people when entering their home. (He greeted the old man warmly.)
- Make room for others at gatherings. (He welcomed the merchant's workers.)
- Be good to guests. (He shared food with Omar despite their disagreements.)
- Forgive others as you would like Allah to forgive you. (He forgave the merchant's past actions.)

The Weight of Words

A young boy, Zayd, often made fun of others. He laughed at their flaws and called them names. His grandfather warned, "Words are like arrows; once released, they cannot be taken back."

One day, Zayd mocked a blind man. The man turned to him and said, "What you see as my weakness is my greatest strength."

Confused, Zayd asked, "How?"

The man smiled. "My blindness has taught me to see with my heart."

Ashamed, Zayd realized the power of his words. From that day, he spoke kindly, turned away from ill speech, and never let arrogance guide his tongue.

Years later, he taught his children, "A kind word heals, but a cruel one wounds forever."

Morals Learned:
- Don't make fun of others. (Zayd learned not to mock people.)
- Don't call others with bad names. (He stopped using hurtful words.)
- Turn away from ill speech. (He avoided gossip and insults.)
- Don't claim yourselves to be pure. (He realized his own flaws.)
- Speak nicely, even to the ignorant. (He changed how he spoke to others.)
- Don't remind others of your favors. (He helped people without boasting.)
- Be patient with your teacher and follow his instructions. (He respected his grandfather's advice.)
- Lower your voice and talk moderately. (He learned to control his tone.)
- Respond to evil with good. (He apologized and became kind.)
- Preach to others in a good and wise manner. (He taught his children about kindness.)

The Journey of Tariq

Prologue: A Life of Gold and Shadows

In the vibrant city of Basra—where bustling bazaars, lively caravans, and the scent of frankincense filled every street—a young trader named Tariq had built a prosperous business. Known for his sharp mind in commerce and persuasive speech, Tariq enjoyed the respect of the wealthy. Yet behind the glittering gold and fine fabrics, his heart was shadowed by pride, impatience, and neglect for deeper values. He often dismissed the poor, spoke harshly without thinking, and boasted of his success without honoring promises or family ties.

One warm afternoon, as sunlight danced upon the marble floors of his opulent home, an elderly scholar named Hamid arrived quietly. With calm eyes and a gentle smile that hinted at decades of wisdom, Hamid said, "Tariq, you have mastered the art of trade, but not the art of living. Come with me on a journey—I will show you the treasures that no wealth can buy."

Tariq, both intrigued and a little defensive, replied, "What could I learn that my success hasn't already taught me?"
Hamid's reply was soft but steady: "Sometimes the hardest lessons are found not in ledgers but along the dusty roads of life."

Reluctantly, Tariq agreed, unaware that each step on this journey would slowly peel away his arrogance and open his heart to truth.

Chapter One: In the Marketplace of Truth

Their journey began in a crowded marketplace. Here, Tariq observed a merchant named Hasan cheating his customers by short-weighing goods. When a customer challenged him, Hasan shrugged dismissively, saying, "Everyone does it; why should I be honest?"
Hamid stepped forward and asked gently, "Would you trust a man who deceives?"
Tariq frowned. "Of course not," he answered, though he wondered if even a successful man might sometimes bend the truth.
"Then why would Hasan lie?" Hamid pressed, and under the watchful eyes of onlookers, Hasan quietly corrected his scales.

Walking further, Tariq and Hamid passed a group of men whispering about a nobleman who, they claimed, secretly hoarded gold. Hamid raised his hand and asked, "Would any of you speak such harmful words to his face?" The murmurs died down instantly, and Tariq felt a stir of regret at the ease with which gossip could destroy a reputation.

Later that evening, while resting in a modest caravan inn, a fellow traveler confided in Tariq a secret business deal. When another merchant later demanded details, Tariq remembered Hamid's words about trust. He held his tongue and instead replied with honesty.

Morals Reflected:
• Do not lie or deceive in trade.
• Avoid backbiting and gossip.
• Keep your trusts and promises.
• (Also remember: Don't spy on others' affairs—a secret is best kept.)

Chapter Two: The Price of Injustice and False Accusations

In the next town, they encountered a harsh ruler known to favor the rich through bribery. One day, a poor servant was falsely accused of stealing a valuable item from a merchant. Tariq saw the fear in the servant's eyes and spoke up, "Surely, we must investigate before punishing an innocent man."
Hamid nodded, adding, "True justice is found in truth and fairness—not in wealth or favoritism."
An inquiry soon revealed that the servant had been framed by someone who wished to profit from the injustice. The ruler, embarrassed and exposed for his corruption, was forced to honor his treaty with honesty.

As they strolled through the town square, Tariq witnessed a group of men ridiculing a traveler's different accent and humble dress. Hamid calmly said, "Allah created differences in color and language to show His artistry. Do not make fun of others."
Tariq's heart ached at the cruelty of such judgment.

Morals Reflected:
• Be just and verify facts before judging.
• Do not take bribes or let injustice flourish.
• Do not mock others or call them by bad names.
• Honor your treaties and respect differences as signs of Allah's wisdom.
• Think good of others instead of assuming the worst.

Chapter Three: Confronting the Ego and the Call to Charity

One cool morning on a dusty road, a beggar approached Tariq, asking humbly for help. Initially, Tariq hesitated, pride whispering that every coin was hard-won. Hamid quietly inquired, "Is your wealth solely yours, or a blessing from Allah meant to be shared?"
Struck by the truth of those words, Tariq reached into his purse and gave the beggar much more than expected, remembering that feeding the poor nourishes both body and soul.

Later that day, in a bustling village square, an arrogant man insulted Tariq publicly. His words were sharp and meant to provoke anger. Tariq felt his temper flare—but then Hamid leaned in, urging, "Restrain your anger. Respond to evil with good."
Taking a deep, measured breath, Tariq simply smiled and wished the man well. The man, humbled by this act of kindness, returned later with a quiet apology.

Morals Reflected:
• Feed the poor and be generous.
• Restrain your anger and respond to evil with good.
• Do not waste resources or opportunities to do right.
• Remember: Do not exult over another's misfortune, and never say what you do not mean.

Chapter Four: The Bond of Family and Respect

In a humble village home, Tariq and Hamid witnessed a young man harshly rebuking his elderly father. "How dare you treat the one who gave you life with such disrespect?" Hamid's stern voice filled the room, and the son's face fell in shame.

That night, Tariq returned to his own modest home and saw his parents waiting with gentle smiles. Realizing he had taken their care for granted, he knelt and embraced them, vowing never to be rude or ungrateful again.

Soon after, they encountered a traveler whose relatives had abandoned him over a trivial dispute. Hamid softly counseled, "Keep your family ties strong, for they are the roots that anchor a man's soul."

Morals Reflected:
- Do not be rude to your parents; honor them.
- Maintain and cherish family ties.
- Keep your oaths and never break promises made to those you love.

Chapter Five: The Power and Respect of Words

As the journey continued through a lively village, Tariq heard harsh words hurled in anger at the marketplace. Hamid stopped him and said, "Turn away from ill speech; words have the power to build or destroy."
That same evening, at a festive gathering, a quarrel broke out between a husband and wife over a trivial matter. Hamid reminded everyone, "Marriage is a sacred trust. Let each speak kindly and make peace rather than harm."
Later, when a young man boasted about his achievements in a way that implied he was pure and above reproach, Hamid gently corrected him, "Do not claim yourselves to be pure. Humility is the mark of true piety."
In all these moments, Tariq learned that speaking nicely—even to the ignorant—and choosing silence over gossip could mend hearts.

Morals Reflected:
• Turn away from ill speech and do not spread gossip.
• Make peace between husband and wife.
• Speak kindly, even to those who know little.
• Do not call others with bad names or mock their efforts.
• Do not remind others of favors you have done; let good deeds speak for themselves.
• And remember, do not call the Prophet or his companions with the same tone you might use for others—show utmost respect.

Chapter Six: Moderation, Humility, and Wise Inquiry

Arriving in a town of extremes, Tariq saw opulent feasts in one corner while the poor struggled for a morsel in another. Hamid softly chided, "Do not be miserly nor extravagant; balance is key in all things."
At a large banquet, a guest peppered the host with endless, unnecessary questions. Hamid advised, "Do not ask unnecessary questions—let silence hold its own wisdom."
While walking along a quiet lane later, Tariq noticed how Hamid's every step was humble, his gait unassuming. "Why do you not walk proudly like others?" Tariq asked. Hamid replied, "Pride belongs to Allah alone. Walk humbly, for humility is strength."

Morals Reflected:
• Do not be miserly nor extravagant.
• Avoid asking unnecessary questions.
• Walk in a humble manner.
• Lower your voice and speak moderately.
• Always be lenient and consult those around you with respect.

Chapter Seven: Trust, Forgiveness, and Fair Dealing

In the crowded market of a new town, Tariq witnessed a scene that shook him. A wealthy merchant publicly reminded a beggar of a past favor, using it to humiliate him. Hamid's voice was firm: "Do not remind others of your favors; let your good deeds be without boast."
Not long after, Tariq saw a woman falsely accused of immorality by a jealous rival. Before the mob could rush to judgment, Hamid declared, "Do not accuse without proof. Let truth be your guide."
In another corner, a man was demanding excessive favors from his neighbors, forgetting the kindness they had shown him. Tariq gently interjected, "Do not ask too many favors; be grateful for what is given."
When a heated dispute arose, Tariq stepped forward, urging, "Make peace between fighting groups." Slowly, tempers cooled, and reconciliation was achieved.

Morals Reflected:
• Do not remind others of your favors.
• Do not accuse without proof.
• Do not ask too many favors from people.
• Make peace between fighting groups.
• Be lenient with those under you and consult them in matters.
• Also, do not wrongly take what is not yours—never take items without right.

Chapter Eight: The Burden and Blessing of Power

Traveling further, Tariq encountered a province where power was misused. A local ruler openly accepted bribes, turning his back on justice. Hamid sternly said, "A ruler must keep his oaths and honor his treaties. Do not take bribes, for leadership is a trust from Allah."

At court, the ruler mocked the beliefs of some citizens. Hamid advised, "Do not insult others' false gods, and always speak gently—even to those whose views differ from yours."

Tariq also noticed that visitors often entered homes without seeking permission. "Seek permission before entering," Hamid reminded everyone, emphasizing respect for privacy.

When a representative of a former enemy arrived with an offer of peace, the ruler hesitated. Hamid declared, "If the enemy seeks peace, then accept it with an open heart; know that enemies can become close friends."

Morals Reflected:
- Do not take bribes.
- Honor your treaties and keep your oaths.
- Do not insult others' beliefs.
- Seek permission before entering someone's room or home.
- Accept peace if offered.
- Remember: Do not wrongly consume the wealth of the vulnerable.

Chapter Nine: A Lesson in Respect, Moderation, and Humble Leadership

On the final leg of his journey, Tariq was invited to a large communal gathering. As he entered the host's home, he remembered to greet everyone warmly —"Greet people when entering their home," Hamid had taught him.
At the event, a respected elder remarked on a minor contribution from a young man. Instead of criticizing, Tariq spoke kindly, "Even small deeds matter," for he had learned not to criticize small contributions of others.
During dinner, someone began to speak harshly about a revered figure. Tariq gently said, "It is not appropriate to discuss slander, especially when our words can wound deeply."
Later, an issue arose among guests regarding an old favor. Tariq recalled the lesson, "Do not ask for repayment for favors, for true kindness is given freely." He also advised a young couple facing marital strife: "Try to make peace between husband and wife, and if ever you need guidance, remember that divorce should be the last resort—handle differences amicably."

Morals Reflected:
• Greet people warmly when entering a home.
• Do not criticize small contributions.
• Avoid discussing slander; speak kindly instead.
• Do not ask for repayment for favors.
• Make peace between husband and wife.
• Treat the wives of the Prophet as you would your own mothers—show utmost respect.
• And remember, do not call someone a disbeliever without knowing their heart.

Chapter Ten: The Final Transformation

After many months on the road—through scorching deserts, verdant oases, and bustling towns—Tariq finally returned to Basra. He was not the proud, haughty trader of old. Instead, his eyes shone with humility, his speech was gentle, and his actions were guided by truth and compassion.

At home, he fulfilled every promise he had made, kept his oaths, and treated every guest with kindness. When an old rival publicly hurled insults at him, Tariq's calm response, "I will not let hatred cause me to be unjust," left the crowd silent.

In council meetings, he never ordered others to do good while neglecting his own duties. He always practiced what he preached, a leader patient with his teachers and consultative with those under him.

He even recalled moments when secret meetings for wrongful purposes were proposed—and firmly rejected them in favor of piety and open dialogue.

In his business, he ensured that no one's wealth was wrongly taken, that no items were acquired without right, and that every transaction was fair.

He treated every person—rich or poor, young or old—with kindness, never raising his voice above that of the Prophet's gentle manner. And when conflicts arose, he punished wrongdoers only as justly as they had wronged others, always exercising patience and compassion.

Final Morals Reflected:
• Keep your trusts and promises and honor your oaths.
• Forgive others as you would like Allah to forgive you.
• Do not let hatred cause you to be unjust.
• Continue spending on those less fortunate.
• Preach to others in a good and wise manner.
• Be patient with your teacher and follow his instructions.
• Do not hold secret meetings for sin—choose piety instead.
• Order others to do good only if you practice it yourself.
• Avoid sitting with those who mock religion until they change their tune.
• And finally, be respectful in every relationship—treat women with honor and never take them by force or reclaim a bridal gift unjustly.

Epilogue: The Legacy of Tariq

Tariq's journey transformed him from a man driven solely by profit into a beacon of truth, justice, humility, and compassion. His life became a living lesson—one that honored every moral teaching and became an enduring legacy for his family and community. His story spread throughout Basra and beyond, inspiring others to seek wisdom over wealth and kindness over cruelty.

In every word he spoke and every act he performed, Tariq embodied the timeless truths taught by Hamid. And so, his path remains a guiding light—a gentle reminder that true success is measured not by gold, but by the goodness within the heart.

A Life Well Lived

Zayd was born in a modest home in Basra, where the scent of freshly baked bread mingled with the metallic tang of his father's blacksmith shop. His father, Harun, was a man of calloused hands and unwavering faith, his back bent from years of honest labor. His mother, Amina, carried the weight of the home with quiet dignity, her presence a source of endless warmth.

Their home was small, their means simple, but it was filled with the kind of love that made a child feel invincible. Zayd grew up watching his parents in awe—his father, whose sweat was a testament to his sacrifice, and his mother, whose soft hands healed every wound, both seen and unseen.

One evening, as the sky turned golden, Harun sat beside his young son, his voice gentle yet firm. "A man's honor is not in his wealth, Zayd, but in the love and prayers of those he serves." Zayd, still a boy, did not fully understand his father's words, but he tucked them away in his heart, where they would stay forever.

As he grew older, his heart was tested. A wealthy merchant from Damascus offered him a position—an opportunity to travel, to earn, to build a name for himself. He felt the tug of adventure, but before making a decision, he turned to his father.

Harun did not command nor forbid. He only said, "Fortune comes and goes, my son. But a son's presence is a blessing that cannot be measured in gold."

Zayd looked at his father's worn hands, at his mother's gentle eyes, and without hesitation, he stayed. He took his father's place in the workshop, his hands learning the dance of hammer and flame. He never let his mother carry a burden alone, tending to her needs before she could even voice them. When his father's hands trembled with weakness, Zayd held them steady. When his mother's feet grew weary, he knelt to slip her sandals on before she could bend down herself.

The years passed, and time, relentless in its course, took first his father and then his mother. Zayd buried them with his own hands, his forehead pressed against the earth, whispering prayers through tears. But his love did not end with their passing.

He continued to honor them—visiting their graves, praying for their forgiveness, and fulfilling every promise they had left behind. He ensured their acts of charity did not cease, arranging for a well to be built in their name so that every sip taken by the thirsty would be a blessing upon their souls.

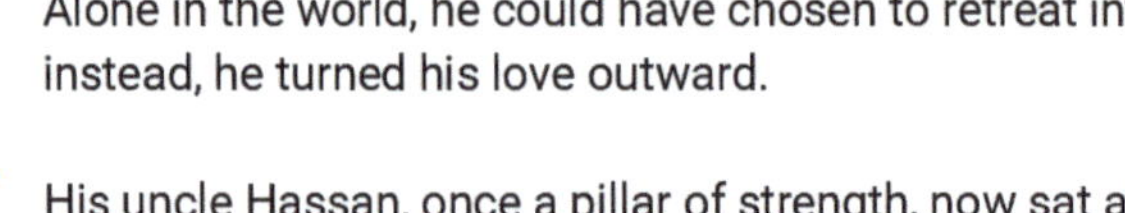

Alone in the world, he could have chosen to retreat into his own grief, but instead, he turned his love outward.

His uncle Hassan, once a pillar of strength, now sat alone in the dim corners of his home, his spirit weighed by old age. Zayd visited him every week, sitting by his side, listening to stories he had heard a hundred times before, laughing as though it were the first time.

His cousin Aisha, widowed and struggling, never had to ask for help. Zayd ensured her needs were met without ever making her feel like a burden.

When his younger cousin Hamza drifted toward bad company, Zayd did not lecture him with harsh words. Instead, he guided him with patience, offering him work in the blacksmith shop, showing him through actions what it meant to be a man of honor.

Disputes arose among his relatives, as they often do when wealth and pride come between family. Inheritance matters, misunderstandings, grudges—things that could have torn them apart. But Zayd was always the first to extend a hand of reconciliation, reminding them that no wealth was worth the loss of kinship.

His kindness did not stop at family.

His neighbors, too, found in him a friend and protector.

Khalid, the elderly man next door, lived alone, his days blending into one another in silent solitude. Zayd made it a habit to check on him, bringing meals, repairing his roof when the rains threatened to seep through, making sure that Khalid never felt forgotten.

One night, the town was gripped by a fierce storm, the winds howling like restless spirits. In the darkness, Zayd heard a desperate knock. It was Rashid, a neighbor who had once wronged him in a business deal. Rashid stood drenched, his family shivering behind him. Their roof had collapsed.

Zayd did not hesitate. He opened his doors, welcoming them as though they had never wronged him. No grudge, no bitterness—only kindness.

Even to those who did not share his faith, he extended the same compassion. Thomas, a Christian man who lived down the street, once faced financial ruin. Zayd helped him without hesitation, asking for nothing in return. "A good neighbor," he reminded him with a smile, "is part of our faith."

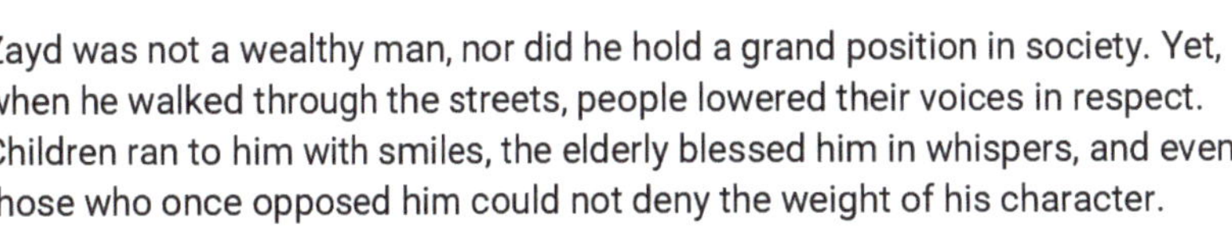

Zayd was not a wealthy man, nor did he hold a grand position in society. Yet, when he walked through the streets, people lowered their voices in respect. Children ran to him with smiles, the elderly blessed him in whispers, and even those who once opposed him could not deny the weight of his character.

As the years passed, his beard turned white, his steps slowed, but his heart remained steadfast.

When his time finally came, the city mourned as though they had lost a father, a brother, a son. His funeral was not just attended by blood relatives, but by neighbors, the poor he had helped, the orphans who had found shelter in his kindness, and even those who had once wronged him.

A young boy, standing beside his father at the burial, looked up at the vast crowd, confusion in his innocent eyes. "Why do so many people love him?" he asked.

His father placed a hand on his shoulder, his voice thick with emotion.

"Because he lived not for himself, but for others. He honored his parents, cared for his relatives, and treated his neighbors as family. That is a life worth remembering."

And so, long after Zayd's body returned to the earth, his kindness remained—a well that never ran dry, a prayer that never ceased, a love that even death could not silence.

The Weight of a Single Date

The streets of Baghdad buzzed with life as the afternoon sun cast golden hues over the city. Merchants called out their wares, children weaved through the crowds, and the scent of fresh bread mixed with the tang of spices in the air. Among the many who roamed the bustling market was Junaid, a man of modest wealth and recognized knowledge. People greeted him with respect, for he was eloquent in speech and well-versed in religious matters. Yet, deep in his heart, there lay an invisible wall—one that separated him from those who toiled in the dust and carried the burdens of society.

To Junaid, laborers, beggars, and street vendors were just fixtures of the city, shadows that moved around him but held no weight in his world. His knowledge, his prayers, and his wealth—though not excessive—made him feel above them. He never harmed the poor, nor did he insult them, but neither did he truly see them.

As he walked through the marketplace, his gaze drifted over the crowds until it rested upon an old man hunched over a small wooden cart. The man's robe, though clean, was tattered and thin, as if it had been mended too many times to hold its original strength. His fingers, darkened with years of labor, carefully arranged the dates before him with surprising gentleness, as if each one was a treasure rather than a common fruit.

Junaid stopped before the cart, his voice carrying the tone of a man accustomed to being served. "How much for a handful of dates?"

The old vendor looked up, his face lined with deep wrinkles, but his eyes—his eyes were alive with warmth. He smiled, as if Junaid were an old friend rather than a passing customer. "A single coin, sir," he replied.

Junaid retrieved a coin from his purse and placed it on the wooden cart. As he turned to leave, the old man's voice stopped him.

Junaid retrieved a coin from his purse and placed it on the wooden cart. As he turned to leave, the old man's voice stopped him.

"Would you like me to weigh the dates properly, or shall I trust your hand to be just?"

Junaid's brows furrowed slightly. "Do you think a man like me would cheat you for a mere handful of dates?"

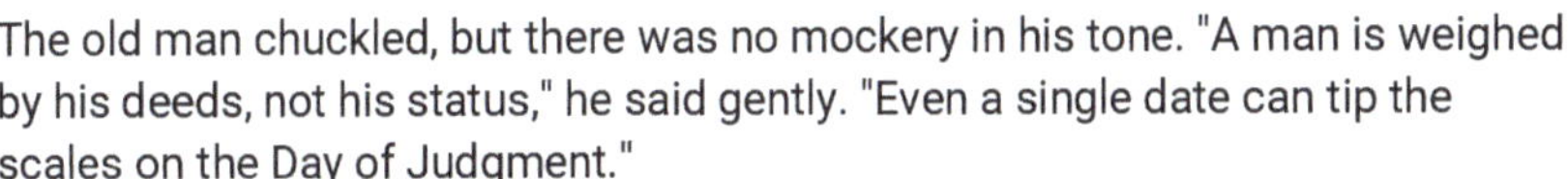

The old man chuckled, but there was no mockery in his tone. "A man is weighed by his deeds, not his status," he said gently. "Even a single date can tip the scales on the Day of Judgment."

For the first time, Junaid truly looked at the man. There was something in his gaze—something that unsettled him. Not challenge, not defiance, but a wisdom that went beyond the boundaries of wealth and knowledge.

"You speak as if you are a scholar," Junaid said, half in jest, trying to mask the strange discomfort in his chest.

The old man smiled again. "No, I am but a seller of dates. But I have seen many scholars walk these streets, and not all of them understand what truly matters."

Junaid felt a sudden need to say something, to correct the old man, to prove his own understanding. But no words came. Instead, he nodded stiffly and walked away, yet the weight of the old man's words followed him like an unseen shadow.

That evening, as Junaid made his way home, he noticed a commotion near the riverbank. A group of laborers had gathered, their faces weary from a day of relentless toil. Among them was a frail man, bent over a sack of grain too heavy for his weakened frame. He tried to lift it, his arms trembling with the effort, but the weight was too much. His fellow workers, though not unkind, were too exhausted to help.

Junaid hesitated. It was not his place to lift sacks of grain. His hands had never known such labor. He was a man of intellect, of prayer, of standing. But then—

A man is weighed by his deeds, not his status.

The words struck him again, as if the old date seller were whispering in his ear.

Before he could stop himself, Junaid stepped forward. "Let me help you," he said, kneeling beside the laborer and grasping the sack. It was heavier than he had expected, the rough fabric pressing into his palms, his arms straining as he lifted it onto the man's back.

The laborer turned to him, eyes wide with astonishment. For a moment, neither spoke. Then, the man placed a trembling hand on Junaid's shoulder. "You are kind, sir," he murmured. "May Allah bless you for this."

Junaid said nothing. He only nodded. But as he walked away, he felt something unfamiliar—a quiet, profound peace. A peace that did not come from being admired or respected, but from something far deeper.

That night, he went to the masjid, where an elderly scholar was narrating stories of the Prophet Muhammad (peace be upon him).

"The Prophet," the scholar said, "never turned away from the poor. When he saw a servant working tirelessly, he did not merely offer kind words—he rolled up his sleeves and worked beside them. When he sat with the destitute, he ate with them as an equal. And when a man claimed superiority over a servant, the Prophet reminded him: No one is greater than another except in piety.

"The true test of faith," the scholar continued, "is not in our prayers or our wealth, but in how we treat those who can offer us nothing in return."

Junaid felt his heart tremble. He thought of the date seller, of the laborer, of his own arrogance. He had been blind, believing knowledge and wealth made him superior. But now he understood: true greatness was in humility, in kindness, in serving others without expectation.

The next morning, he returned to the marketplace, seeking the old date seller. But the stall was empty. Frowning, he turned to a nearby merchant.

"Where is the old man who sold dates here?"

The merchant looked at him with a solemn expression. "He passed away last night. May Allah have mercy on him."

Junaid felt a strange heaviness in his chest. He had not even known the man's name. Yet, he had changed his heart. He whispered a prayer for the old man, for his wisdom, for the single date that had tipped the scales of his soul.

From that day forward, Junaid walked through the streets of Baghdad with different eyes. He no longer passed the poor as if they were invisible. He lifted burdens—not just of grain, but of hardship. And in doing so, he found something he had never known: contentment in the eyes of the downtrodden, and the weight of a single date upon his soul.

For in the end, it is not our wealth, but our kindness, that will tip the scales.

The Weight of a Gaze

The streets of Damascus were always alive with voices—merchants calling out their prices, travelers bargaining, the murmur of people sharing news. Among the crowd walked Nabeel, a young man of keen intelligence and ambition. He was a student of Islamic law, admired for his knowledge and eloquence in debates. But beneath his growing reputation, there was an unspoken struggle—one that he had not yet recognized within himself.

Nabeel understood the rules of modesty and interaction between men and women. He could recite the legalities effortlessly: who was a mahram, who was not, the limits of speech and conduct. But like many, he saw these boundaries as formalities, external rules rather than matters of the heart. It was not until an ordinary afternoon in the bustling marketplace that he came to understand the true weight of his actions.

The sun was beginning to dip toward the horizon when Nabeel found himself near a fabric shop, waiting for a friend. As he stood there, his eyes casually wandered over the people passing by. That was when he saw her—a young woman, modestly dressed, speaking with the elderly shopkeeper. There was nothing unusual about her, yet he found his gaze lingering.

She was not his mahram. He knew that. But he was only looking, he told himself. There was no harm in that.

Then, just as she turned to leave, her eyes lifted for the briefest moment—meeting his. And in that instant, he felt something unexpected: not excitement, not admiration, but shame.

Her expression did not show anger, nor did she scowl. Instead, there was something far more powerful in her face—discomfort, disappointment, and quiet dignity. It was as if she had seen through him, not just the glance, but the intention behind it. Without a word, she lowered her gaze and walked away.

Nabeel felt his throat tighten. He had read countless texts about haya—modesty—but never had he felt its weight as he did now.

That evening, he sought out his teacher, an elderly scholar known for his wisdom. After the night prayer, he approached him, hesitant but eager to understand what had unsettled him so deeply.

"Teacher," Nabeel began, "I have always known that lowering the gaze is an obligation. But today, I failed to do so, and for the first time, I felt... ashamed. Not just because I was seen, but because I truly understood that I had wronged someone."

The scholar nodded, his face calm. "Tell me, Nabeel, do you know why Allah commands men to lower their gaze?"

"To guard against temptation," Nabeel answered without hesitation.

The scholar smiled slightly. "That is true, but it is not the only reason. Lowering the gaze is not just about avoiding temptation—it is about honoring others, protecting their dignity, and disciplining the soul. It is an act of sincerity, not just an external rule."

Nabeel was silent, reflecting.

The scholar continued, "When a man looks at a woman who is not his mahram, he does not just take a moment from her—he takes her sense of security. A glance can be as heavy as a touch if it is unwelcome. And when a woman dresses modestly, she is trusting society to respect her dignity. Will you be among those who honor that trust, or those who violate it?"

Nabeel felt the weight of those words settle in his heart. "I never thought of it that way," he admitted.

The scholar nodded. "That is because many see modesty as a restriction, rather than a protection. But a true believer does not follow rules blindly—he understands their purpose. Do you wish to be a man of strength, Nabeel?"

"Of course," he replied.

"Then control your gaze," the scholar said firmly. "For true strength is not in conquering others, but in conquering the desires of your own soul."

That night, Nabeel lay awake, replaying the moment in the marketplace. He thought of the young woman's expression, the unspoken message in her eyes. She had been a stranger, yet she had taught him a lesson that no book had conveyed so deeply.

The next day, as he walked through the city, he noticed things he had not before—the way men's eyes followed women as they passed, the way casual conversations stretched beyond necessity, the way laughter and teasing blurred the lines of respect.

He saw how something as small as a glance could change the way a woman walked, how she adjusted her scarf, how she avoided eye contact to shield herself.

For the first time, he truly understood.

From that day on, Nabeel changed—not just in action, but in his heart. He lowered his gaze not as an empty gesture, but as a sincere act of respect. He spoke to women with measured words, ensuring his tone remained appropriate and his intentions pure. He treated his mother and sister with renewed reverence, understanding that how he honored them reflected his character.

And years later, when he married, he cherished his wife not as a possession, but as a trust from Allah—one that he would protect, not just in her presence, but in her absence as well.

For he had learned that a man is not defined by how many eyes admire him, but by how many hearts trust him.

And true honor is not in seeking attention, but in guarding dignity—his own, and that of others.

The Weight of a Word

The night air was cool as Rayyan walked home through the narrow streets of his neighborhood. The city of Basra was quiet at this hour, the laughter of merchants and the clatter of carts having faded with the setting sun. But in Rayyan's mind, one voice echoed louder than all the others—the laughter of his friends, ringing in his ears like a heavy drum.

Tonight had been no different from any other. They had gathered outside the mosque after Isha prayer, talking and joking, their words flowing freely. Rayyan had always been quick-witted, known among his friends for his sharp tongue. With him, no conversation was ever dull—he always had a joke, a remark, a playful insult to keep the laughter going.

And tonight, the target had been Idris.

Idris was a quiet young man, a tailor's apprentice, with an awkward gait and a timid nature. He rarely spoke unless spoken to, and when he did, his words were slow and careful. The others often teased him, and Rayyan was the best at it.

Tonight, he had imitated Idris's slow speech, exaggerating his stutter, making the others roar with laughter. He had called him The Silent Donkey—a name that had stuck for weeks. Idris had smiled faintly, as he always did, lowering his head. But before he left, Rayyan had noticed something—a glimmer in his eyes, a flicker of hurt that vanished as quickly as it appeared.

At the time, he had ignored it. But now, as he walked home alone, it stayed with him.

That night, sleep refused to come. Rayyan tossed and turned, the words of his jokes replaying in his mind. He had not meant harm—it was only fun. Wasn't it?

A deep unease settled in his chest. Something about tonight felt different.

Unable to silence his thoughts, he rose before Fajr and made his way to the mosque. The city was still wrapped in darkness, the streets empty except for a few early risers heading for prayer.

Inside, he found the elderly scholar, Sheikh Hamid, sitting in the dim light of the mosque, his fingers moving over his prayer beads.

Rayyan hesitated, then approached. "Sheikh," he said softly, "may I ask you something?"

The old man smiled, nodding. "Of course, my son. What troubles you?"

Rayyan hesitated before speaking. "My friends and I... we joke often. Last night, I made fun of a friend, but now I feel uneasy. I didn't mean to hurt him, but..." He paused, struggling to find the right words. "Do words carry such weight, even if they are spoken in jest?"

The sheikh's expression darkened slightly. He placed the prayer beads aside and gestured for Rayyan to sit.

"My son," he said, his voice gentle yet firm, "have you read the words of Allah?"

Rayyan nodded. "Yes, of course."

"Then you know that Allah says in the Qur'an: 'O you who have believed, let not a people ridicule another people; perhaps they may be better than them... And do not insult one another and do not call each other by offensive nicknames. Wretched is the name of disobedience after faith. And whoever does not repent —then it is they who are the wrongdoers.' (Surah Al-Hujurat 49:11)"

Rayyan's breath caught in his throat. He had heard the verse before, but now, it felt like it was directed at him alone.

The sheikh continued, "Do you know what the Prophet (ﷺ) said about mocking others?"

Rayyan shook his head, his heart heavy.

"The Messenger of Allah (ﷺ) said, 'A believer is not one who taunts, curses, speaks obscenely, or ridicules others.' (Tirmidhi)"

The sheikh paused, letting the words settle. "Tell me, Rayyan—what do you think hurts more, a wound on the skin or a wound on the heart?"

Rayyan lowered his gaze. "The heart," he whispered.

"Indeed," the sheikh nodded. "A wound on the body heals. A wound caused by words? It stays. Some wounds last a lifetime."

A lump formed in Rayyan's throat. He thought of Idris—his quiet nature, his forced smiles, the way he never responded to their jokes. Had he been hurting all along?

"Sheikh," Rayyan said, his voice tight, "what if... what if I have already caused such wounds?"

The old man placed a reassuring hand on Rayyan's shoulder. "Then seek forgiveness—from Allah, and from the one you have hurt. Do not delay. A heart can harden with time, but it can also soften if approached with sincerity."

Rayyan nodded, his chest tightening with guilt. He knew what he had to do.

The sun had just begun to rise when Rayyan found himself outside the tailor's shop. Idris was already there, setting up his work for the day.

Taking a deep breath, Rayyan stepped forward. "Idris," he called softly.

The young man looked up, surprised. "Rayyan?"

Rayyan swallowed his pride. "I... I need to talk to you."

Idris nodded hesitantly.

Rayyan took a deep breath. "I have wronged you," he admitted. "I've made jokes at your expense, I've called you names, and I never stopped to think how it might have hurt you." He looked Idris in the eyes. "I am ashamed. And I ask for your forgiveness."

Idris blinked, clearly taken aback. He was silent for a moment, then let out a small breath. "I... I never said anything because I didn't want trouble," he admitted. "But, yes... it hurt."

Rayyan's heart sank.

Idris gave a small, tired smile. "But I forgive you."

Relief flooded through Rayyan. "Thank you," he said, his voice filled with gratitude. "I promise, I will never mock you again. Or anyone else."

Idris nodded. Then, after a pause, he said, "You know, Rayyan... you're funny even without hurting people."

Rayyan smiled, feeling lighter than he had in years.

From that day on, he changed. He still joked, still laughed—but never at someone's expense. And whenever he saw others making fun of someone, he stepped in—not as a participant, but as a voice of reason.

For he had learned that words are not just sounds carried by the wind. They are weighty, they leave marks, and they can either uplift a heart or break it.

And a believer—one who truly fears Allah—chooses his words carefully, knowing that on the Day of Judgment, every word will be accounted for.

For in the end, laughter fades, but the pain of a careless word can last a lifetime.

The Weight of Two Worlds

The city was alive with motion, yet Sufyan felt strangely distant from it. He sat at his desk in the university library, the pages of his economics textbook open in front of him, but his mind was elsewhere.

His phone buzzed. A message from his study group: "Meeting at 7. Don't be late."

He sighed, rubbing his temples. Exams were just a week away, and the pressure was mounting. Every moment not spent studying felt like a moment wasted. He had plans—big plans. A career in finance, a stable life, success. That was the goal, wasn't it?

And yet, there was a lingering discomfort in his heart, a weight that he couldn't quite explain.

For weeks now, he had been skipping his evening gatherings at the mosque, telling himself he'd make up for it after exams. His Qur'an, once read daily, now sat untouched at his bedside. Even his du'as had become hurried, rushed between lectures and late-night revisions.

"Just until exams are over," he told himself. "Then I'll make time."

But a small voice in his mind whispered: What if time runs out first?

Shaking off the thought, he turned back to his books, drowning himself in numbers and theories, trying to silence the quiet unease that had begun to settle deep in his chest.

The night before his final exam, Sufyan found himself restless. He had studied relentlessly, pushing himself to the edge of exhaustion. But as he lay in bed, staring at the ceiling, something gnawed at him.

What was it all for?

A verse from the Qur'an echoed in his mind:

"But you prefer the life of this world, while the Hereafter is better and more lasting." (Surah Al-A'la 87:16-17)

He exhaled sharply. Of course, the Hereafter was important. But surely, he was doing the right thing by focusing on his studies first? Success in this world was necessary too, wasn't it?

Sleep didn't come easy that night. And when it finally did, it brought with it a dream—one that would change everything.

Sufyan found himself standing in a vast, open plain. The sky above him stretched endlessly, neither day nor night, just an eerie, timeless glow. A strange silence surrounded him, broken only by a distant, rhythmic sound—like the ticking of a clock.

He turned, searching for its source, and his breath caught.

Before him stood two towering scales. One side held a heap of books, certificates, and stacks of wealth, glittering with earthly success. The other side was nearly empty—save for a small, flickering light, barely strong enough to be seen.

As he watched, the scales trembled. Slowly, they began to tip. The weight of his worldly pursuits pulled heavily, dragging the other side into the air. The flickering light—his prayers, his Qur'an, his deeds—seemed insignificant in comparison.

Panic surged through him. He rushed forward, trying to add something to the lighter side. He grasped for prayers he had skipped, for acts of kindness he had postponed, for the Qur'an he had neglected. But his hands passed through them like mist. They weren't there.

A voice—calm yet firm—echoed around him.

"And what is the life of this world except the enjoyment of delusion?" (Surah Al-Hadid 57:20)

Sufyan fell to his knees, his heart pounding.

Had he been chasing an illusion?

The ticking grew louder. The scales continued to tip.

Then—everything went black.

Sufyan jolted awake, his heart hammering against his ribs. His room was dimly lit by the faint glow of his phone screen, still open to an email about an upcoming business deal. He ran a trembling hand over his face, trying to shake off the weight of the dream.

But it wasn't just a dream. It felt like a warning.

He glanced at the time—3:45 AM. Fajr was approaching, yet his body felt heavy. He had missed Tahajjud again. He had told himself he would pray more, seek Allah's closeness, but each day passed in a blur of meetings, deadlines, and ambitions.

His eyes landed on the framed certificate on his desk—his degree, proof of years of dedication and hard work. Next to it, a dusty Qur'an sat untouched. The contrast struck him like a blow.

"What have I been building?" he whispered to himself.

He had spent years preparing for the future—securing wealth, a career, and a name for himself. But what of the future that was certain? The one that stretched beyond this fleeting life?

Another verse echoed in his mind:

"But you prefer the worldly life, while the Hereafter is better and more enduring." (Surah Al-A'la 87:16-17)

A lump formed in his throat. Have I been preferring the lesser over the greater?

Determined, Sufyan rose from his bed. The floor was cool beneath his feet as he made his way to the prayer mat. He picked up the Qur'an, brushing away the layer of neglect.

As he stood in prayer, the world outside seemed to fade, and for the first time in a long while, he felt something shift within him.

The dawn broke gently, casting a golden hue over the city skyline. Sufyan sat by the window after Fajr, the Qur'an open before him. The words felt different today—not just verses to recite, but guidance he had long overlooked.

"The life of this world is nothing but play and amusement. But far better is the home of the Hereafter for those who are righteous. Will you not then understand?" (Surah Al-An'am 6:32)

He closed his eyes, the weight of the verse sinking in. He had spent his years chasing success, consumed by meetings, investments, and future plans. But what was he truly preparing for?

His phone buzzed on the table. A message from a client, another business proposal. Normally, he would have responded immediately. Today, he hesitated.

A soft knock on his door pulled him from his thoughts. His mother peeked in, her face gentle with a smile.

"Beta, will you come to visit your uncle today? He hasn't been well."

Sufyan's mind flickered to his packed schedule—calls, contracts, endless obligations. But another thought cut through—how many obligations to the world had he placed above his obligations to his soul?

He nodded. "I'll come, In shā' Allāh."

His mother's smile deepened. "Alhamdulillah. It will make him happy."

As she left, Sufyan looked back at his phone, then at the Qur'an in his hands.

"Balance," he murmured. "I must find balance before it's too late."

The midday sun hung high as Sufyan made his way through the narrow streets to his uncle's home. It had been months since he last visited. Work had always been an excuse, but deep down, he knew—it wasn't just work. It was his priorities.

When he entered, the small home felt warm despite its simplicity. His uncle, a frail man with deep lines of wisdom on his face, lay on a wooden cot, his eyes bright with recognition.

"Sufyan, my boy," his voice was weak but filled with warmth. "It has been a long time."

Sufyan lowered his gaze, guilt pressing against his chest. "Forgive me, Uncle. I should have come sooner."

The old man chuckled softly. "Time is a strange thing, my son. We chase it, yet it is never in our hands."

Sufyan sat beside him, listening as his uncle spoke of life, of people he once knew, of prayers he never missed, of wealth that came and went but never truly stayed.
"Your father, may Allah have mercy on him, was a man of balance," his uncle said suddenly. "He built his business, yes, but he built his akhirah alongside it. I remember—whenever a deal was made, he would give a portion in charity before even celebrating. And before every major decision, he would seek knowledge—because he feared making wealth his master instead of his servant."

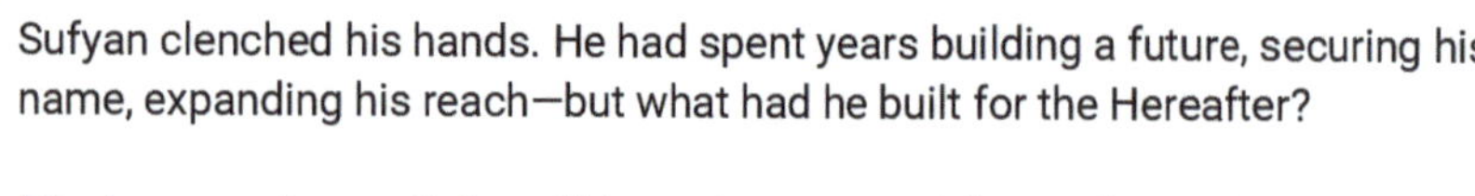

Sufyan clenched his hands. He had spent years building a future, securing his name, expanding his reach—but what had he built for the Hereafter?

"You're a good man, Sufyan," his uncle continued. "But tell me, if you were called back to Allah tomorrow, would you be ready?"

The question landed heavier than any business deal, any contract, any lost opportunity.

Would he be ready?

Sufyan remained silent, staring at the patterns on the old woven rug beneath his feet. The air felt heavier now, the weight of his uncle's question pressing deep into his soul.

Would he be ready?

The thought unsettled him. He had spent years strategizing, investing, ensuring his worldly affairs were in order. But when had he last sat and truly reflected on his standing with Allah? When had he last wept in sujood, asking for guidance instead of success?

His uncle watched him, a knowing look in his weary eyes. "You remind me of myself when I was younger," he said with a faint smile. "Running, always running. Thinking that if I just reached the next goal, I would finally find peace. But peace never comes from the world, Sufyan. It is only found in the remembrance of Allah."

Sufyan exhaled slowly. "But is it wrong to work hard, Uncle? To build, to achieve?"

The old man shook his head. "No, my son. Islam never tells us to abandon the world. The Prophet (ﷺ) was a merchant before he was a leader. The Companions worked, traveled, and traded. But their hearts... their hearts were anchored in the Hereafter. The world was in their hands, not in their hearts."

He paused before continuing, his voice turning softer. "It is like a boat, Sufyan. A boat belongs on water, but if water enters it, it sinks. Similarly, you must live in the world, but if the world enters your heart, it will drown you."

Sufyan looked up, his uncle's words striking something deep within him. He had always believed he was in control—of his business, his future, his time. But now, he saw the truth. Time was slipping through his fingers, and he had spent too little of it preparing for what truly mattered.

His uncle smiled knowingly. "Balance, my son. That is what Islam teaches us. To work, but also to worship. To plan for this life, but also for the one that never ends."

Sufyan nodded slowly, a new determination settling in his heart. It wasn't too late. He could still set things right.

The night breeze was cool as Sufyan walked home, his uncle's words lingering in his mind like an echo he couldn't shake. The streets were quiet, the world around him slowing down, yet inside, he felt a storm of thoughts.

He had always assumed he was doing well—fulfilling his obligations, praying when required, giving charity when reminded. But was it enough?

He thought of his investments, the long hours spent perfecting deals, ensuring profits. Every detail was meticulously planned, no effort spared. But when had he last planned for the eternal life to come? When had he last spent a night in prayer, investing in his soul the way he did for his business?

As he neared his home, the faint call to prayer resonated through the streets. It was the pre-dawn prayer, Fajr. Sufyan hesitated, standing at the doorstep. The masjid was just a short walk away.

For a fleeting moment, he considered going inside, washing up, and going straight to bed. He had a long day ahead—meetings, calls, responsibilities. But then, another thought crept in.

Hadn't he spent late nights closing business deals? Hadn't he sacrificed sleep to ensure his profits? Then why did waking up for prayer feel like an inconvenience?

He turned away from his home and made his way toward the masjid. The doors were open, the soft glow of lights spilling onto the ground. A few men were already inside, their voices low in dhikr.

Sufyan stepped in, the cool marble beneath his feet sending a strange sense of calm through him. He performed his ablution, feeling the cold water wash away more than just dust—it felt as if it was cleansing his heart, too.

As he stood in prayer, the Imam began reciting:

"But you prefer the worldly life, while the Hereafter is better and more lasting." (Surah Al-A'la, 87:16-17)

Sufyan closed his eyes, the words piercing straight into his soul. It was as if they had been sent just for him, a direct response to the battle waging within his heart.

Tears welled up in his eyes. For the first time in years, he truly felt the weight of his choices.

And in that moment, Sufyan knew—he had spent enough time chasing the temporary. It was time to start preparing for the eternal.

The morning sun had risen by the time Sufyan left the masjid, its golden light spilling across the quiet streets. But something within him felt different, as if he had stepped into a new world—not one that had changed around him, but one that had shifted within him.

He walked home slowly, his heart still heavy with thought. The past years played in his mind—how he had dedicated himself to success, to building a future, to securing comfort for himself and his family. Yet, he had neglected to secure the only future that truly mattered.

As he entered his home, his wife greeted him with a warm smile. "You're back later than usual," she noted, setting down a cup of tea.

"I went to the masjid for Fajr," he said, sitting down.

She raised her eyebrows in surprise but said nothing.

For the next few days, something within Sufyan remained unsettled. He still handled his business, still managed his affairs, but his heart was elsewhere. He found himself drawn more to the masjid, more to the Qur'an, more to moments of reflection.

One evening, he sat across from his uncle again, the same man who had unknowingly planted the first seed of doubt in his mind.

"Uncle," he said slowly, "I've been thinking about what you said. About the world and the Hereafter."

The old man smiled knowingly. "And?"

Sufyan exhaled. "I have spent years planning for my future, yet I never planned for my real future. I thought I was balanced, but I was only deceiving myself."

His uncle nodded. "Balance is not giving both equal weight, my son. Balance is giving each its due. The world will end, but the Hereafter is endless. Which one deserves more of our effort?"

Sufyan looked down, deep in thought.

That night, as he lay in bed, he whispered a du'a he had long forgotten:

"O Allah, do not let me be among those who remember You only in words, but let my heart, my actions, and my soul remember You in every step I take."

The next morning, he rose before dawn—not for business, not for wealth, but for something greater. For the first time in years, he felt truly alive.

For he had finally understood: success in this world is temporary, but success in the Hereafter is eternal. And only a fool would invest everything in what is fleeting, while neglecting what will last forever.

The Illusion and the Reality

The glow of the screen flickered across Ibrahim's face, casting long shadows on the walls of his dimly lit room. His fingers danced across the controller, every movement precise, every action instinctive. His teammates' voices crackled through his headset—shouting strategies, calling for backup, celebrating victories.

Outside, the call to prayer echoed through the streets, its solemn melody drifting through his open window. His mother's voice followed soon after, gentle yet firm.

"Ibrahim, it's time for Maghrib."

"Just one more round, Mama," he murmured, barely registering her words as he dodged an on-screen ambush.

It was the same, every evening. The same game, the same excuses, the same neglect of time slipping through his fingers like sand.

By the time he finally powered down his console, the night was deep, the silence in his room almost unnerving. He reached for his phone, scrolling mindlessly through posts, videos, messages. Everything felt fleeting—an endless stream of content, yet nothing truly settled in his mind. The laughter of influencers, the debates in comment sections, the perfectly curated lives of strangers—it was a world both vast and hollow.

And then, just as he was about to move on to another video, his eyes landed on something different. A hadith shared by an old friend, Yusuf:

"There are two blessings which many people waste: health and free time." (Bukhari)

Ibrahim froze. He had heard these words before, but they had never felt so personal.

A strange unease settled in his chest. For the first time in a long time, he noticed the weight in his limbs, the dull ache in his eyes from staring at the screen for too long. He thought of his father, who had once taken him to the masjid every evening, his firm yet warm hand on his shoulder as they walked together. He thought of the afternoons spent outside, kicking a ball with Yusuf and the others, the sweat and exhaustion feeling more fulfilling than any virtual victory.

Now, his world had shrunk. Four walls. A screen. A connection to thousands of people—and yet, a growing distance from himself.

Restless, he tossed his phone aside and stood up, his body stiff from hours of sitting. He walked to the window and gazed outside. The mosque lights still glowed in the distance.

A quiet longing stirred within him. Without overthinking it, he grabbed his jacket and stepped outside.

The night air was cool, carrying with it the distant hum of the city. As he neared the mosque, he noticed a familiar figure—Yusuf, leaning against the gate, scrolling through his phone.

Ibrahim hesitated. He hadn't spoken to Yusuf in months. Their conversations had become shorter, their meetings rarer. Somewhere along the way, their friendship had faded, replaced by endless virtual interactions that never truly filled the gap.

Yusuf looked up and, for a brief moment, seemed surprised. Then, a slow smile spread across his face. "Ibrahim?"

Ibrahim rubbed the back of his neck. "Yeah... just thought I'd take a walk."

Yusuf chuckled. "A walk? That's new."

"Yeah, well," Ibrahim exhaled. "Felt like I needed some air."

Yusuf studied him for a moment, then nodded towards the road. "Come on, let's walk."

They walked in silence for a while, the sounds of the city fading behind them. Finally, Yusuf broke the quiet.

"You know, you used to be the one dragging me outside. What happened?"

Ibrahim sighed. "Life happened, I guess. Games, social media... it's just how things are now."

Yusuf smirked. "Is it? Or is it just what we've settled for?"

Ibrahim shot him a questioning look.

"I used to be the same," Yusuf admitted. "Glued to my screen, thinking I was connected to everything. But the more time I spent online, the more... disconnected I felt. From my family, my friends, even myself."

Ibrahim frowned. "Gaming isn't all bad. It's fun. It helps me relax."

"Fun is good," Yusuf agreed. "Even the Prophet (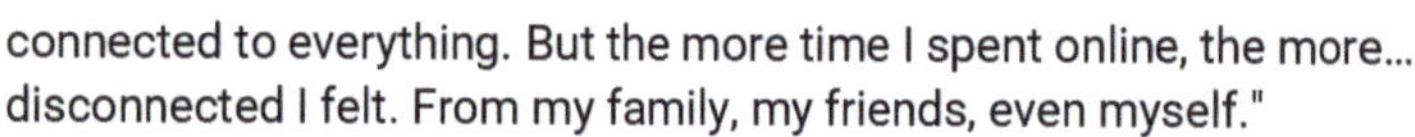) encouraged recreation—horse riding, swimming, archery. But tell me, when was the last time you did something that actually made you feel alive? Not just entertained, but fulfilled?"

Ibrahim opened his mouth, but no answer came.

Yusuf continued, his tone softer now. "Look, I'm not saying to quit gaming. But balance, Ibrahim. We weren't created just to kill time. If we're not careful, time will kill us first."

The words hit deep.

Ibrahim exhaled slowly. "So what changed for you?"

"I started looking for something real," Yusuf said. "I joined a local football group, spent more time at the masjid, picked up reading again. And for the first time in years, my mind felt clear."

Ibrahim nodded absently, his mind swirling with thoughts.

That night, as he lay in bed, he reached for his phone—but this time, he didn't open a game or social media. Instead, he searched for something different. Something real.

And for the first time in a long time, he felt a sense of clarity.

For he realized—the real world, with all its struggles and beauty, was far richer than anything a screen could offer.

The following days passed in a quiet struggle. Ibrahim still found himself reaching for his controller out of habit, still heard the familiar buzz of notifications calling him back to the endless stream of content. But something had shifted.

Each time he powered on his console, Yusuf's words echoed in his mind: "When was the last time you did something that made you feel alive?"

One evening, as he sat in front of his screen, headset in place, his team waiting for him to join the match, his fingers hovered over the buttons.

The game world flickered to life—colors, movement, strategy—but suddenly, it all felt... hollow.

With a sigh, he pulled off the headset and turned off the console.

Instead, he picked up his phone and sent a message.

Ibrahim: What time's the game tomorrow?

The reply came almost instantly.

Yusuf: Finally. 5 PM. Don't be late.

The next afternoon, Ibrahim laced up his old football shoes, the ones he had tossed into his closet months ago. As he stepped outside, the sun felt different on his skin—warmer, more real.

The field was buzzing with energy when he arrived. Yusuf was already there, stretching. A few familiar faces turned to him in surprise.

"Ibrahim?!" One of the boys laughed. "Did you get lost on your way to the digital world?"

Ibrahim grinned. "Figured I'd see if I still know how to kick a ball."

The game started, and within minutes, Ibrahim felt the rush—the burn in his muscles, the thrill of the chase, the exhilaration of movement. When he scored, a surge of real joy coursed through him. No high-score screen, no virtual leaderboard—just real people, real laughter, real moments.

After the game, as they sat on the grass catching their breath, Yusuf nudged him. "So? How does it compare to sitting in front of a screen?"

Ibrahim smirked. "It's... different."

"Better?"

Ibrahim hesitated, then nodded. "Yeah. Better."

Yusuf leaned back on his elbows, watching the sunset. "You know, there's nothing wrong with gaming, Ibrahim. But life isn't meant to be lived through a screen. We were created for more than that."

Ibrahim exhaled. "I get it now."

For the first time in years, he felt awake. The weight of wasted time still sat heavily on his shoulders, but for the first time, he wasn't adding to it. He was choosing something better.

That night, he didn't reach for his console.

Instead, he picked up a book.

And with each passing day, the virtual world faded a little more, replaced by something richer—something real.

Days turned into weeks, and Ibrahim's routine slowly transformed. His console, once the centerpiece of his room, gathered dust. His phone, once a constant source of distraction, now held fewer notifications. The habit of mindlessly scrolling through feeds, consuming content without thought, had loosened its grip.

But it wasn't easy.

There were nights when boredom crept in, tempting him to return to his old ways. He'd feel the urge to escape into a game, to lose himself in the rush of competition, the thrill of victory. The internet was still there, just a few taps away, offering endless entertainment, a world where time disappeared without notice.

Yet, each time he felt himself slipping, something stopped him—something stronger than mere discipline.

One evening, after Maghrib prayer, he sat across from his father at the dinner table. It had been a while since they had spoken at length. The past few years had been filled with absent-minded conversations—his father asking how school was, Ibrahim mumbling a response while half-listening, distracted by his phone.

But tonight was different.

His father studied him for a moment, then smiled. "You seem… different these days."

Ibrahim hesitated, then shrugged. "I guess I've been thinking a lot."

"About?"

"Life… how I spend my time. How much I've wasted."

His father nodded thoughtfully. "Time is the one thing we can never get back, Ibrahim. That's why the Prophet ﷺ said: 'There are two blessings which many people waste: health and free time.' (Bukhari)"

Ibrahim lowered his gaze. He had read the hadith before, but it struck differently now.

His father continued, "Entertainment isn't haram, son. But when it becomes an escape, when it pulls us away from reality, from responsibility, from the people who matter—that's when we need to ask ourselves: is this worth it?"

Ibrahim swallowed hard.

For years, he had justified his habits. It's just gaming. It's just social media. Everyone does it. But what had he gained? Hours spent on leaderboards that meant nothing, conversations filled with memes but lacking meaning, a world that existed only behind a screen.

"Do you regret it?" his father asked gently.

Ibrahim thought for a moment. "I regret how much I let it control me," he admitted. "But... I think I needed to go through it to understand."

His father smiled. "Then don't waste the lesson."

That night, as Ibrahim lay in bed, he thought about everything he had missed— the moments with family, the friendships that had faded, the dreams he had abandoned in favor of quick entertainment.

And he realized something.

The internet and gaming weren't the enemies. The problem had never been the tools—only how he had used them.

It wasn't about quitting completely. It was about balance.

And for the first time, he was ready to find it.

In the weeks that followed, Ibrahim rebuilt his life—not by cutting off everything, but by realigning his priorities.

He still played games, but in moderation. No more all-night sessions, no more skipping prayers for "just one more match." If he played, it was after fulfilling his responsibilities, and never at the cost of real-life connections.

He still used the internet, but with intention. No more endless scrolling, no more falling into the trap of mindless consumption. If he went online, it was to learn, to connect meaningfully, to benefit rather than waste.

One afternoon, as he walked past the local mosque, he noticed a group of younger boys huddled together, their faces lit by the glow of a phone screen. He recognized the excitement in their eyes—it was the same look he once had.

He hesitated, then approached. "What are you guys watching?"

One of the boys, no older than twelve, grinned. "A new gaming tournament. These guys are insane!"

Ibrahim smiled. "Yeah? You know, I used to play a lot too."

The boys looked at him with curiosity. "Used to?"

"Yeah. Still do sometimes, but I realized something—no matter how many levels I beat, how many matches I won, none of it actually made my life better. Not really."

The youngest frowned. "But gaming is fun."

"It is," Ibrahim agreed. "But you know what's even better? Living a life where you're not just watching someone else succeed, but actually building something real for yourself."

The boys fell silent, considering his words.

One of them spoke hesitantly, "So... what do you do now?"

Ibrahim chuckled. "Plenty. I started reading more, training in martial arts, spending time with my family. I still have fun, but now, when I look back at my day, I actually feel like I did something that mattered."

They exchanged glances, as if weighing his words against their own habits. Finally, one of them asked, "Do you think we waste too much time?"

Ibrahim's smile softened. "That's not for me to say. But ask yourself—when you look back in ten years, will you be proud of how you spent your time? Because Allah swears by time in the Qur'an: 'By time, indeed mankind is in loss, except for those who believe, do righteous deeds, and encourage truth and patience.' (Surah Al-Asr 103:1-3)"

The boys nodded slowly, and as Ibrahim walked away, he saw one of them lock his phone and pocket it.

For the first time in years, Ibrahim felt something new—purpose.

He had spent so long lost in a digital world, forgetting that life was happening beyond the screen. But now, he was back, and he wasn't looking back.

The internet would always be there. The games would always be there.

But so would real life.

And this time, he chose to live it.

Notes